From the authors of *American Clocks and Clockmakers*

# PRICE GUIDE TO

*Antique Clocks*

## ROBERT AND HARRIETT SWEDBERG

Published by

**krause
publications**

700 East State Street, Iola, WI 54990-0001

Please, call or write us for our free catalog of antiques and collectibles publications. To place an order or receive our free catalog, call 800-258-0929. For editorial comment and further information, use our regular business telephone at (715) 445-2214.

Library of Congress Catalog Number: 98-84444
ISBN: 0-87069-760-9
Printed in the United States of America

# Table of Contents

# Introduction to Collecting and Pricing Clocks

Clocks are wonderful to collect, display and enjoy. There is a diverse variety of clocks available to buy. Some owners specialize. For example, they seek only old clocks, those made by certain makers, such as Seth Thomas or Eli Terry. Original or untampered examples are highly sought. Other collectors might like calendar clocks or the later novelty examples that feature "bobbing" or "swinging" dolls or nursery creations. Some select products made by a favorite clock maker.

Prices vary somewhat, however. Don't be shy about asking questions. Most "clock people" are glad to talk to neophytes. A leading question might be, "Is this clock all original?" Also a buyer wants to know if the clock runs well and is accurate. Clocks often require keys to open the door or to wind the mechanism. Are the keys available? A case that is in good condition is naturally more appealing and valuable than one that is not.

As you search for clocks, use caution because some of those that are for sale, particularly at large auctions, are "marriages." This means that parts from several clocks have been combined to make one clock. Buy from a reputable dealer so you can return your purchase if it does not meet the standards that have been established for it.

We have attempted to check and recheck the information we have used in this book; we have found, even among established authorities, there are sometimes disagreements regarding dates, makers and clock names. In our research, we have encountered many such discrepancies. An example concerns the mid 17th century Christiaan Huygens who invented the clock pendulum. Sometimes his first name is listed with only one "a"— Christian. Two other spellings of his last name appeared as "Huyghens" or "Huijghens."

Dates differ also. For example, one source lists Eli Terry's residence in Terryville, according to his obituary

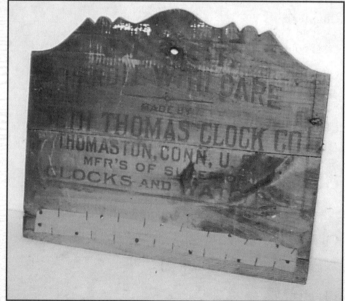

on Feb. 21, 1852, which contradicts the fact that the Terrysille Post Office was established on Dec. 22, 1831, and it was not until sometime after 1872 that the "s" was dropped and the town became Terryville. We're certain, too, that we will not be errorless.

Our books attempt to assist novices who seek to learn more about collectible and antique articles. We use no museum or catalog pictures. Our photographs are all from private homes, antique or clock shows, conventions or shops. During the long process of compiling this book, we have learned a great deal about clocks from the collectors and dealers who have shared their knowledge with us. We sincerely express our appreciation to these people.

The authors of this book do not determine the prices of the clocks which are depicted. Therefore, neither the authors nor the publisher assume the responsibility for losses that readers might possibly incur as a result of consulting this guide. Prices are set by the knowledgeable and capable members of the NAWCC (National Association of Watch and Clock Collectors), reliable dealers and also collectors who enjoy the diverse variety of timepieces and clocks that are available.

# *Acknowledgments*

The authors sincerely thank the following collectors and dealers who assisted us in obtaining photographs and information for this book (as well as those clock collectors who did not wish to be listed):

Annawan Antique Alley
Mary Wheeler
Annawan, Illinois

Antique America
Cheryle Fry
Davenport, Iowa

Antique & Specialty Center
Don and Sharon Hanebuth
Anchorage, Alaska

Marion and Vera Blevins

Richard and Norma Broline

Bill and Dora Brubaker

Chuck Cline

Heartland Antique Mall
Pam Ropp
Geneseo, Illinois

Pastor Troy C. Hedrick

Scott Helmich

J. & S. Antiques & Mall
Jim and Sandy Boender
Manlius, Illinois

Shirley Kilgard

David and Emily Lewis
Specializing in Kroeber clocks
Western Illinois

Michael and Patricia Lowe

Bill and Sandy Mittelstadt

Peerless Antiques & Auctions
Chris Wojtanowski
Rock Island, Illinois

Terry and Gretchen Poffinbarger

Dennis and Barbara Roberts

Ken Russell
Antique Clocks & Clock Repair
Lacon, Illinois

Barry and Lori Snodgrass

Patrick Thomas
Antique Clocks
Dorking, England

Mariam Thornton

# Chapter 1

# An Overall View of Clock Types

Pictured in this chapter are 27 examples of the different types of clocks that are shown and priced throughout this book. These selected sample photographs will enable you to see the wide variety of clock styles that are depicted and priced in this book.

*Alarm clock:* New Haven Beacon in original box, 4-1/2" x 6"—$90.

*Advertising clock*: Waterbury oak store regulator with Coca-Cola advertisement on bottom tablet, time and strike (most of these are time only); top tablet is original but bottom isn't, 16" wide, 36" high—$350.

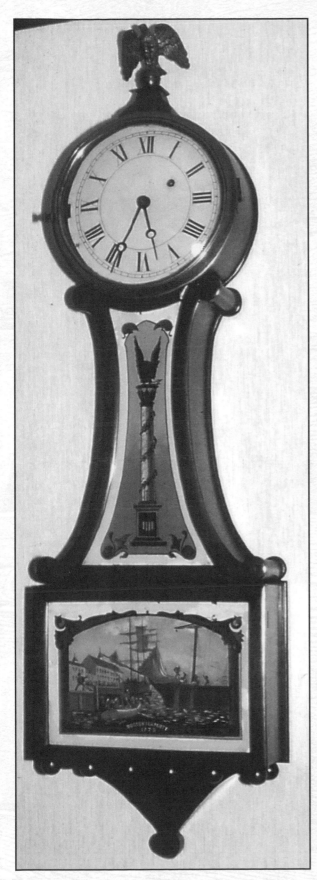

*Bracket clock*: Unmarked, probably German, mahogany bracket clock, circa 1900, that is sitting on a matching bracket; double fusee movement, time and Westminster chimes, circa 1900, 10" wide, 14" high—$850.

*Banjo clock*: Chelsea walnut banjo clock, circa 1890, time only with single weight-drive, made in Boston, 39" high—$3,200.

***Gallery clock***: Seth Thomas walnut gallery clock, 15-day, time only, 18" dial, 25-1/2" outside diameter—$1,500.

**Cabinet clock**: Ansonia "Cabinet Antique" polished mahogany cabinet clock with antique brass trimmings, French sash, finials and porcelain and brass face, eight-day, time and strike, 9-1/4" wide, 20" high—$2,000.

**Calendar clock**: Ithaca "#8 Shelf Library," walnut perpetual calendar clock, with burl inlay, 12" wide, 26-1/2" high—$1,000.

**Carriage clock**: French brass carriage clock with glass panels, folding handle, 3" wide, 6" high—$575.

**Crystal regulator clock**: Seth Thomas "Empire #29" crystal regulator, circa 1905, simulated mercury pendulum, beveled-glass panels, bronze top and base, rich gold body, 14-day movement, 9" wide, 17" high—$750.

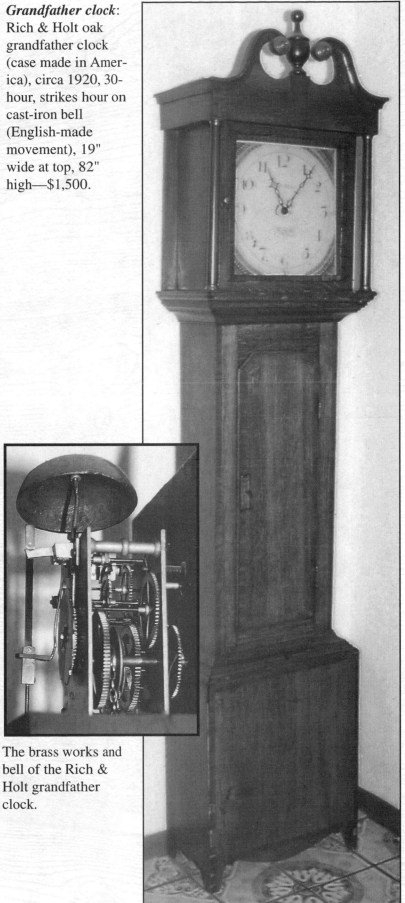

*Grandfather clock*: Rich & Holt oak grandfather clock (case made in America), circa 1920, 30-hour, strikes hour on cast-iron bell (English-made movement), 19" wide at top, 82" high—$1,500.

The brass works and bell of the Rich & Holt grandfather clock.

*Cuckoo clock*: Black Forest walnut cuckoo clock with three weights, cuckoo on hour and quail every 15 minutes, late 1800s, 19" wide, 25" high—$185.

***Mantel clock***: Seth Thomas mantel clock with black-enameled adamantine finish, brass dial, feet and lion heads at each end, dated Sept. 7, 1880, 17" wide, 11-1/2" high—$200.

***Metal-front shelf clock***: New Haven metal-front shelf clock with Cupid figure, 4-1/2 wide, 7" high—$130.

*Oak shelf clock*: Sessions oak shelf clock, circa 1910, Mission-style with brass Arabic numerals, eight-day, time only, 8" wide, 14-1/2" high—$165.

*Lighthouse shelf clock*: French 19th century lighthouse shelf clock with porcelain and brass construction and barometer on back, Doulton's signed base, 18" high—$2,000.

**Kitchen clock**: Seth Thomas "#2" oak kitchen clock, in a six-set series, brass decorations, eight-day, time, strike and alarm, 15" wide, 23-1/2" high—$250.

**Octagon clock**: Ansonia oak, "Regulator B," drop octagon clock, circa 1890, time only, 17" wide, 32" high—$425.

*OG shelf clock*: Chauncey Jerome walnut veneer OG shelf clock, circa 1885, 30-hour, weight-driven, 26" high—$175.

*Walnut shelf clock*: New Haven walnut shelf clock, incised lines and applied decorations, eight-day, time and strike, 14" wide, 21-1/2" high—$225.

***Porcelain shelf clock***: Ansonia "La Cheze" Royal Bonn porcelain shelf clock, eight-day, time and strike, 8" wide, 10" high—$450.

***Papier-mâché shelf clock***: Jerome & Co. papier-mâché shelf clock with mother-of-pearl inlay and fusee movement, eight-day, time and strike, 11" wide, 14" high—$700.

**Statue shelf clock**: Ansonia statue shelf clock with fisherman and hunter figures, double mercury-style pendulum, 14" wide, 15" high—$695.

**Steeple shelf clock**: Waterbury rosewood Gothic-steeple shelf clock, circa 1870, 30-hour, time and strike, 19-1/2" high—$195.

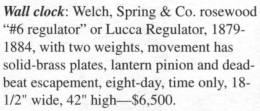

***Triple-decker shelf clock***: Birge, Mallory and Company triple-decker shelf clock, circa 1845, brass strap movement invented by Joseph Ives, painted wood dial, original bottom glass tablet, eight-day, weight-driven, 17" wide, 38" high—$650.

***Wall clock***: Welch, Spring & Co. rosewood "#6 regulator" or Lucca Regulator, 1879-1884, with two weights, movement has solid-brass plates, lantern pinion and dead-beat escapement, eight-day, time only, 18-1/2" wide, 42" high—$6,500.

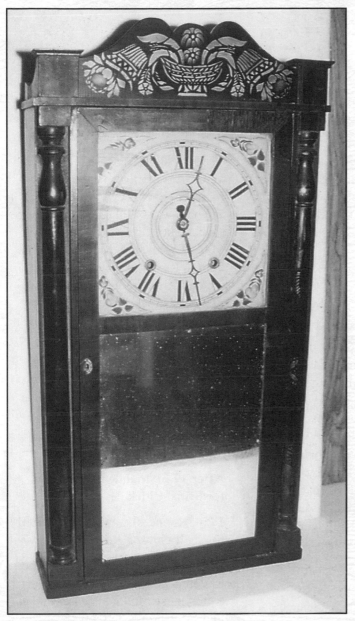

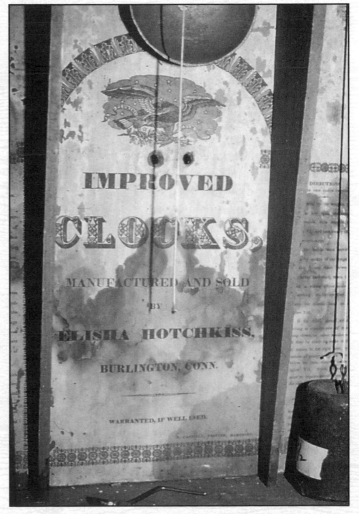

*Mirror shelf clock*: Elisha Hotchkiss mahogany mirror shelf clock, dated 1835, 30-hour, time and strike, weight-driven with wooden dial and movement, top repainted but all original—$300.

Label for Elisha Hotchkiss mirror shelf clock. The label reads, "Improved Clocks Manufactured and Sold by Elisha Hotchkiss, Burlington, Conn. Warranted if well used."

# Chapter 2

# A Brief History of Clockmakers

The historical events that follow is our attempt to present a succinct review of horological history. We have tried to show facts as accurately as our research permits, keeping in mind, as most researchers know, that sources sometimes differ on dates, names and other facts relevant to clock history.

**1380**: Italy produced the first domestic clocks.

**1386**: England's earliest known public clock was installed at the Salisbury Cathedral.

**1500**: The mainspring was invented by Peter Henlein of Nurnberg.

**1525**: Fusee was invented by Jacob the Czech.

**1530**: Screws for metal work became available.

**Circa 1584**: Galileo (1564-1642) was an astronomer, physicist and college professor who was born in Pisa, Italy. Galileo was a 20-year-old college student (according to some sources, slightly younger) when, on a visit to the city's cathedral, he watched a suspended lamp swinging to and fro. Timing it with the beat of his pulse, he discovered that a short swing moved slowly while a long one moved more rapidly. Because of this, the time taken for the completion of a swing back and forth was the same for both.

**1607**: The first successful settlement in North America was Jamestown in what is now the state of Virginia.

**1620**: The Pilgrims, a group of people who left England to seek religious freedom in the New World, established Plymouth Colony in what is now the state of Massachusetts.

**1640**: The manufacture of Black Forest clocks began.

**Early 1600s**: Among these colonists who settled in 1607 and 1620 were skilled workers, including those with clockmaking knowledge. They made clocks one at a time, relying on England for their supplies.

**Circa 1650**: The first tower clock was completed in Boston.

**1660**: The balance or hair-spring came into use.

**1657**: Back in the Old World, a Dutch scientist, Christiaan Huygens, created the first pendulum based on Galileo's observations. The pendulum's swing back and forth served as a clock's regulating mechanism. This inventor's name is spelled in various ways by different authors. Most spell his first name with one "a" while his last name has been seen as "Huijghens," "Huygens" or "Huyghens."

**1673-1771**: George Graham's two essential contributions to clockmaking were the dead-beat escapement and the mercurial compensation pendulum.

**1680**: Second hands made their first appearance.

**Late 1600s**: A London-made grandfather clock cost about $57. Its case was a choice of walnut or ebony, and it had fancy carvings and gilted metal-applied decorations.

**1726**: Ebenezer Parmelee of Guildford, Connecticut, built a clock that was installed in the town's church tower.

**1730**: The German clockmaker Anton Ketterer made his first cuckoo clock.

**1738-1770**: In Lancaster, Pennsylvania, Abraham Le Roy made quality tall-case clocks with brass dials. In colonial days, a few women were clockmakers. One of them, Anna Maria LeRoy, the daughter of Abraham LeRoy, had the opportunity to watch her father at work and later produced clocks. She married Wilmer Atkinson in 1749. The dials of her clocks from 1750-1760 bore his name.

**1740**: The first cuckoo clocks were made in the Black Forest region of Germany, but it took several decades before this style of clock became popular.

**After 1740**: Mahogany was used for British clock cases.

**1750**: Round dials were introduced for shelf clocks.

**1749-1796**: In the years before the Revolutionary War began, David Rittenhouse of Dutch descent inherited some books and tools from his uncle. This may have aroused his interest in mechanics. He began making high quality clocks in 1749. After the former English colonies became the United States of America, Rittenhouse came to know and work with American leaders including Benjamin Franklin and Thomas Jefferson. He made astronomical instruments and started the first observatory in the United States. Rittenhouse served as the director of the U.S. Mint in Philadelphia from 1792-1795. He was recognized as a scientist as well as a maker of quality clocks.

**1760**: The four Willard brothers from Grafton, Massachusetts, were clockmakers. The first one to take up this trade, around 1760, was Benjamin who worked in various places including Grafton.

**Pre-1775**: In colonial America, craftsmen made clocks to order, one at a time. This was an expensive process and metal and glass were scarce. Brass movements were fashioned by hand with simple tools. Boston, New York and Philadelphia were all centers for the production of the tall-case floor clocks, better known as grandfather clocks. During this time, there were several hundred clockmakers at work in the various colonies.

**1775-1783**: Clockmaking in the colonies came to a halt during the Revolutionary War as clockmakers joined the fighting forces or made equipment for the soldiers. Many clockmakers became gunsmiths.

**1790-1812**: Gideon Roberts, a Revolutionary War veteran, possibly was the first to use mass-production methods in his Bristol, Connecticut, clock factory where both hanging wall clocks and tall-case clocks were made. Many were sold to out-of-state buyers. Since brass clock-works were expensive, he created his own wooden movements and used painted paper dials. Some clocks were made without cases. Since the pendulum could be seen easily as it swung back and forth, the descriptive phrase "wag on the wall" became an appropriate name for these caseless clocks. Of course, a buyer could make a case or have a wood worker fashion one and then he would own a conventional clock. Roberts assembled his 30-hour tall-case clocks with their wooden movements in groups of 10 or more at a time. This innovation speeded up the production process and made less costly clocks available to buyers.

**1793**: Following the completion of his apprenticeship, Eli Terry began making clocks near Plymouth, Connecticut.

**Circa 1800**: The production of wooden clocks began in the United States.

**Circa 1800**: Gideon Roberts owned an assembly plant in Richmond, Virginia.

**1802-1840**: Simon Willard made about 4,000 clocks during this time span. One was the banjo clock which sold for $35. Early 19th century clockmaking was a problem because metal was scarce and the supply of glass was limited. Everything had to be done by hand and the craftsman and his apprentice used the simplest tools in their work-namely a hammer, drill and file.

**1802-1860**: Banjo clocks were made in the United States.

**1802**: Simon Willard patented his "Improved Timepiece" later called "banjo" because of its shape. Originally, most examples were time only. This popular clock style has been copied consistently over the years.

**1807-1809**: The Jefferson Embargo limited the importation of material from English factories.

**1807-1810**: Eli Terry contracted to make an unheard of 4,000 hang-up clock movements at $4 each in three years' time. The water power-driven machines he designed produced identical interchangeable wooden parts for inexpensive (grandfather type) clock works.

Silas Hoadley and Seth Thomas worked for him. Terry is credited with introducing the factory system of mass production. This helped start the factory system in the United States; inexpensive clocks, made in quantities, became available to the public.

**Circa 1810-1813**: Seth Thomas and Silas Hoadley bought Eli Terry's Plymouth clock shop. Thomas sold out in 1813 and Hoadley continued in business.

**1811-late 1830s**: Six Ives brothers, including Joseph and Chauncey, were involved in the clock industry.

**1813**: Seth Thomas set up his own shop in Plymouth Hollow, Connecticut, where he became a prolific clockmaker.

**1809-1810**: Eli Terry established a partnership with Seth Thomas.

**1812**: Eli Terry set up an experimental shop that produced low-

Seth Thomas mahogany pillar mirror shelf clock with Seth Thomas on the dial, time and strike, 10-1/2" wide, 16-1/2" high—$165.

priced wooden shelf clocks.

**1816**: Eli Terry patented a pillar-and-scroll shelf clock with a 30-hour wooden works that evolved from his plain box-type case. For a short time, Chauncey Jerome made clock cases for Eli Terry.

**Circa 1818**: Joseph Ives made a brass clock movement with steel plates.

**1820**: The manufacture of side-column clocks began.

**1820-1830**: Circumventing Terry's patent, other companies varied the pillar-and-scroll clock, frequently using brass eight-day movements.

**1822**: Joseph Ives of Bristol patented a looking-glass clock, but Aaron Willard claimed that Massachusetts makers had been using looking-glasses to add variety to clock fronts for some 25 years.

**Circa 1822**: The "Lighthouse" clock was patterned after the Eddystone Lighthouse at Plymouth, one of the earliest in England. This clock was introduced by Simon Willard, It was eight-day, weight-driven and had an alarm. A glass dome covered the clock.

**1822-1855**: Birge was associated with the clockmakers Ives, Case, Gilbert, Fuller and Peck.

**1824**: Chauncey Jerome formed a partnership with his brother, Noble, and Elijah Darrow for the manufacture

of clocks. The firm was called Jeromes & Darrow. About 1825, Jerome patented a "bronze looking glass clock" with a 30-hour wooden movement, using a mirror instead of a tablet and bronze-colored pilasters. Jerome specialized in case-building and usually bought his movement from others.

**Circa 1825**: Before 1825, Joseph Ives had learned how to make rolled brass. He moved to Brooklyn, New York, where he stayed briefly and invented the wagon spring to power a clock. The wagon

Chauncey Jerome (he invented the case and movement of OG clocks) mahogany OG, brass dial, circa 1845, 30-hour, time and strike, 15-1/2" wide, 26" high—$300.

spring is a series of flat-leafed arched springs that resemble those

used in wagons.

**Circa 1825-1920**: "OG" or "ogee," S-curved, veneer-framed clocks were made and sold widely throughout the 95-year period. They were prolonged best sellers.

**1828**: Elias Ingraham settled in Bristol as a cabinet and case maker of clocks; Mark Leavenworth of Waterbury, Connecticut, made wooden movements for clocks; Marsh, Gilbert & Company operated a clock business in Bristol.

**1830**: Eli Terry's son, Silas B. Terry, patented a method for tempering coiled springs so they could be produced inexpensively; Irenus Atkins, a Baptist minister, started a clock factory at Bristol, converting a church into a factory as no other building was available for his purpose.

**After 1830**: Rolled brass became more available for clock movements. Chauncey Jerome gave his brother, Noble, an idea for replacing wooden clock works with inexpensive rolled-brass movements. Some authorities feel that Chauncey copied Joseph Ive's mirror clock and his brass movement.

**1831**: Elias Ingraham founded the E. Ingraham Company; Terrysville Post Office was established on Dec. 22, 1831, in honor of Eli Terry; J.C. Brown made clocks in Bristol.

**Circa 1832**: Daniel Pratt Jr., was a clockmaker in Reading, Massachusetts.

**1831-1837**: Burr & Chittenden were making clocks in Lexington, Massachusetts.

**1832-1836**: Boardmand and Wells made a great number of wooden-movement shelf clocks, using as many as four factories at one time.

**1833**: Elisha Brewster started a factory at Bristol, which came to be known as Brewster & Ingraham.

**1836**: James S. Ives of Bristol received a patent for a brass coiled clock spring.

**Prior-1837**: Clocks were used for bartering purposes.

**1837 and later**: These were prosperous years with factories and mass production well established.

**1837-1843**: The firm of Birge & Mallory experienced prosperous times in its manufacture and sales of clocks.

**Circa 1840s**: Elias Ingraham, Bristol, designed a sharp Gothic clock popularly called a "Steeple" clock.

**1840**: Spring-driven clocks were introduced.

**1840-1842**: Jerome shipped a lot of his brass clocks to England. The British authorities bought all. He sent another lot and they bought all of these. When the third shipment arrived, they realized that a really inexpensive and reliable clock was being imported and they allowed them to be sold.

**1842-1859**: These marked the partnership years of Edward Howard and David P. Davis whose principal manufacture was the banjo clock.

**1842-1849**: H.C. Brown became J.C. Brown & Company and also used the name Forestville Manufacturing Company.

E. Ingraham walnut-stained simple calendar shelf clock, eight-day, time and strike, 15" wide, 19-1/2" high—$250.

Brewster & Ingraham burled walnut Gothic shelf clock, brass springs, replaced tablet and hands, eight-day, time and strike, 10-1/2" wide, 19" high—$400.

**1840-1850**: All American clocks were weight-driven until the mid 19th century because the United Stated did not have rolling mills that were capable of producing spring steel.

**1843**: The partnership of Boardman & Wells ended and Wells and other clockmakers formed the Bristol Company

**1844**: John Birge and Thomas Fuller formed a partnership that lasted until the death of Fuller in 1848; Elias and Andrew Ingraham who were brothers formed a partnership with Elisha C. Brewster and started producing the steeple clock which rapidly gained in popularity (this innovation soon replaced the large three-section Empire case, known as a "triple decker," which was a popular item among Connecticut clockmakers of the 1830s); Chauncey Jerome had 12 brass clock factories in Bristol and a case factory in New Haven, Connecticut.

**1845**: When one of Jerome's Bristol factories burned down, 50,000 to 75,000 brass movements were destroyed.

**1846**: Jerome moved his entire operation from Bristol to New Haven.

**1848**: A Howard Tower clock was installed in a church in New Hampshire.

**1847**: The depression stopped American clockmaking and was the end of the wooden clock movement.

**1849**: American Clock Company, New York City, was organized as a

Forestville Mfg. Co. mahogany OG, circa 1848, made by J.C. Brown, circa 1848, eight-day, time and strike, weight-driven, 17" wide, 29" high—$450.

American Clock Co. (address on label is #3 Cortlandt, New Broadway) metal mantel clock with mother-of-pearl inlay, brass dial, eight-day, time and strike (winders below dial), 8-1/2" wide, 16" high—$400.

large depository to sell clocks made by various companies. The company issued catalog of wares.

**1850**: Weight-driven clocks were gradually replaced by spring-driven ones; The Ansonia Clock Company was established in Ansonia, Connecticut, by Anson Phelps; The American Clock Company was organized.

**Circa 1850**: Brass-coiled springs were largely replaced by better and cheaper steel springs; Nicholas Muller was at work in a foundry in New York City where he made iron-front clocks.

**1850-1860**: The production of tall clocks had generally ceased.

**1851**: Samuel Emerson Root was at work in Bristol where he made some marine-type movements.

**Circa 1851**: The Wm. L. Gilbert Clock Company, Plymouth, was incorporated; Hiram Camp started the New Haven Clock Company in New Haven; John H. Hawes of Ithaca, New York, patented the first known simple-mechanism calendar clock.

**After 1853**: Many patents were issued for calendar clocks.

**1854**: A fire at the Ansonia Clock Company forced the company to move to Phelp's Mill under the new name of Ansonia Brass and Copper Company.

Ansonia "Sovereign" polished mahogany crystal regulator, mercury pendulum, beveled glass, visible escapement, eight-day, half-hour gong strike, 10-1/2" wide, 18-1/2" high—$3,400.

W.L. Gilbert statue clock of an archer stringing his bow, brass decorations and two cherubs at the base, open escapement, porcelain face, eight-day, time and strike, 10" wide, 33" high—$3,000.

Waterbury "Parlor #98" porcelain shelf clock, porcelain dial, eight-day, time and strike nickel-plated movement, 9" wide, 11" high—$450.

Ithaca Calendar Clock Company walnut perpetual-calendar shelf clock with ebony-applied decorations and turned columns. The dates of the month are in gold around the outer rim of the bottom tablet, and the days and months are on rotating tubes behind the tablet, eight-day, time and strike, 10" wide, 20" high—$4,000.

**1855**: The New Haven Clock Company took over Jerome Manufacturing Company and continued to use the Jerome name; John Briggs of Concord, New Hampshire, received a patent for a clock escapement called "Briggs Rotary"; The Ansonia Bobbing doll was patented; The E&A Ingraham clock plant in Bristol burned.

**1857**: The Waterbury Clock Company began operations in Waterbury; Elias Ingraham began The E. Ingraham Clock Company in Bristol.

**1858**: Solomon Spring owned a clock company.

**1859**: The Ansonia Swinging doll was patented; Seth Thomas died; Westminster chimes were introduced.

F. Kroeber cast-iron black-enameled mantel clock, circa 1898, gilted decorations, eight-day, time and strike, 12-1/2" high—$275.

**Circa 1863**: F. Kroeber manufactured clocks in New York City, made fine cases and often altered purchased movements.

**1863-1868**: L.F. and W.W. Carter made calendar clocks.

**1864**: Mozart, Beach & Hubbell patented a perpetual-calendar clock that needed to be wound only once a year; E.N. Welch of Bristol consolidated the clock companies he purchased under the name of E.N. Welch Manufacturing Company.

**1865**: When the Ithaca Calendar Clock Company was established, it used Henry B. Horton's perpetual roller-type calendar clock patent.

**1866**: Plymouth Hollow became Thomaston, Connecticut, to honor the (Seth) Thomas name. As a result, clock labels were changed to "Thomaston."

**1867**: A battery-operated clock was marketed; Alfonso Broadman, Forestville, Connecticut, made a simple calendar clock with two rollers, one for the month and the date and the other for the day of the week.

**1868**: The Welch, Spring & Company partnership was organized, specializing in the manufacture of regulator and calendar clocks; Joseph K. Seem's patent showed the way to attach three small disks to the back of an existing clock dial, making it a simple calendar clock.

**1868-1893**: Parker & Whipple Company operated in Meriden, Connecticut.

**1869**: Celluloid, a flammable, plastic, was developed. It was later used on clock cases to simulate tortoiseshell, amber, onyx and other materials.

**1870s-1880**: George Owen, Winsted, Connecticut, had a small shop that later merged with Gilbert and Company.

**1871**: Daniel Gale, Sheboygan, Wisconsin, patented an astronomical calendar clock dial.

**1872**: Terrysville, Connecticut became Terryville; Joseph K. Seem obtained a patent for a perpetual calendar roller mechanism that could be fitted on top of an existing clock when space permitted.

**1878 or before**: Ansonia clocks were marked "Ansonia, Connecticut."

**1878 or later**: Ansonia clocks were marked "New York."

**1879**: Ansonia Clock Company moved to Brooklyn, New York. Shortly after the move, a fire destroyed the factory.

Welch, Spring & Co. "Gerster" walnut parlor clock (named after Hungarian soprano, Etelka Gerster), four decoratively turned columns, Patti movement, eight-day, time and strike, 12-1/4" wide, 18-1/2" high—$1,400.

**Circa 1880**: Nicholas Muller's Sons made fancy shelf-clock cases of iron and bronze; a song that gave a name for the long-case clock said, "My grandfather clock was too tall for the shelf, so it stood ninety years on the floor."

**1880**: H.J. Davis made an illuminated alarm clock.

**1881**: Joseph K. Seem was granted a patent that improved his original 1872 perpetual calendar mechanism.

**1882**: The Macomb Calendar Clock Company was formed in Illinois. The company used Seem's 1881 Calendar Clock patent.

**1881-1885**: Yale Clock Company, New Haven, advertised novelty clocks.

**1883**: The Macomb Calendar Clock Company went out of business; A.D. Clausen patented the "Ignatz" (flying pendulum) clock; Benjamin Franklin, Chicago, patented a perpetual calendar clock mechanism that could be attached to an existing clock by cutting a hole in its dial.

**1885**: The Sidney Advertising Clock Company, Sydney, New York, developed a large wall clock on which advertising drums turned every five minutes.

**1886-1916**: Darche Electric Clock Company, Chicago and Jersey City, New Jersey, made battery-alarm timepieces.

**Circa 1888**: The Self Winding Clock Company, New York City and Brooklyn, made battery-powered and electric clocks.

**1890**: Edward P. Baird & Company was established in Plattsburgh, New York. It used Seth Thomas works

and papier-mâché for the body.

**Circa 1890**: Jennings Brothers Manufacturing Company of Bridgeport, Connecticut, made metal clocks.

**1891-1897**: Henry Prentiss of New York City received various patents for calendar mechanisms that ran for one year after being wound.

Parker Clock Co. alarm clock with brass statue of a girl carrying a basket on top, 30-hour, time only, 7" wide, 13" high—$750.

**1893**: The Parker Clock Co., Meriden, Connecticut, took over Parker & Whipple. The firm made small pendulum desk clocks, round alarm clocks and novelty clocks.

**1895**: Western Clock Manufacturing Company began in La Salle, Illinois.

**1896-1900**: Edward P. Baird & Company moved to Evanston, Illinois, where it made wooden-case clocks with metal dials rimmed with embossed and painted advertisements.

**1897**: Chelsea Clock Company operated in Chelsea, Massachusetts. The company's output included auto and ship clocks, as well as those for the home.

**Late 1800s**: Simplex Company of Gardner, Massachusetts, made time recorders and time clocks; Decalcomania transfers were common on clock tablets.

**1902**: John P. Peatfield of Arlington, Massachusetts, patented a perpetual calendar clock with a spring-driven mechanism that was wound yearly.

**1903**: Sessions Clock Company, Bristol-Forestville, Connecticut, bought E.N. Welch Manufacturing Company.

**1908**: The Loheide Mfg. Co. made a black-case metal-trimmed shelf clock that contained a slot-machine arrangement that took $2.50 gold pieces. The patent number 883,886 dates the clock to 1908.

**1910**: "Big Ben" alarm clocks were made.

**1915**: "Little Ben" alarm clocks were made.

**Circa 1917**: Paul Lux of Waterbury founded the Lux Clock Manufacturing Company and produced many novelty clocks. He used molded wood cases. His clockmaking pursuits included the name De Luxe.

**1929**: International Business Machine Corporation (IBM), Endicott, New York, was organized; Ansonia Clock Company's equipment and materials were purchased by the Soviet government and moved to the Soviet Union.

**1931**: August C. Keebler of Chicago founded the August C. Keebler Company, which marketed Lux Clocks, including the pendulettes that he sold to large mail-order companies. He did not make clocks, but his name was sometimes used on Lux Clocks.

**1936**: Westclox, a trade name, became the new name for Western Clock Manufacturing Company; Hammond Clock Company of Chicago was in operation.

Lux Shmoo clock in its original box, never used; Li'l Abner and Daisy Mae are pictured on the box, 30-hour, time only, spring-driven, 4" wide, 7" high—$250.

# Chapter 3
# *Representative Clocks from Smaller Clockmakers*

Most of the following companies or individual clock makers produced clocks in small quantities and they are not as prevalent on the market as the products of the major companies. For this reason, we have put them together in this chapter of the book so you would be able to see the contributions made by these tradesmen. In most cases their clocks will be found among those from the early 19th century when a great deal of experimentation was being done in an attempt to produce better and more efficient clocks.

Clocks manufactured by the major clock companies include Ansonia Clock Company, the E. Ingraham Company, E.N. Welch Manufacturing Company, Eli Terry, William L. Gilbert Clock Company, New Haven Clock Company, Seth Thomas and the Waterbury Clock Company. Examples of their timepieces will be pictured in the sections covering the various types of clocks.

An alphabetical list of these smaller clock makers is presented below, along with the name of the clock that will be pictured.

| Name of company/maker | Clock shown |
| --- | --- |
| American Clock Company | Iron front |
| Baird | Advertising |
| E.M. Barnes | Transition |
| Chauncey Boardman | Steeple |
| W. Boardman | Transition |
| Brewster & Ingraham | OG |
| Birge, Mallory & Co. | Triple-decker |
| J.C. Brown | Steeple |
| L.F. & W.W. Carter | Calendar |
| E.O. Goodwin | Transition |
| Hopkins & Alfred Clock Co. | Transition |
| Howard Electric Clock | Shelf |
| L. Hubel | Advertising |
| C. & L.C. Ives | Transition |
| Jerome & Company | Transition |
| Chauncey Jerome | OG |
| William S. Johnson | Double OG |
| F. Kroeber Clock Co. | Porcelain Missing |
| Lux Clock Company, Inc. | Mantel |
| Macomb Calendar Clock Co. | Calendar |
| Elisha Manross | OG |
| Manross Prichard & Co. | OG |
| Mitchell Vance & Co. | Iron front |
| Parker of Connecticut | Iron front |
| Roswell-Kimberly | Shelf |
| Russell and Jones | Shelf |
| Southern Calendar Clock Co. | Calendar |
| Elmer Stennes | Banjo |
| Terry & Andrews | OG |
| Welch, Spring & Co. | Calendar |
| M. Welton | OG |
| Western Clock Mfg. Co. | Statue |

American Clock Company metal case shelf clock, multi-colored with birds and flowers on case, 30-hour, time and strike, spring-driven, 13" wide, 16" high—$300.

Baird advertising wall clock, circa 1896, eight-day, time only, spring-driven, 31" high—$1,500.

Label from E.M. Barnes transition shelf clock with old wooden movement. Label reads, "Improved clocks manufactured and sold by E.M. Barnes, Bristol, Conn. at wholesale and retail. Warranted if well used."

Chauncey Boardman mahogany veneer mirror tablet steeple clock, circa 1845, 30-hour, reverse fusee movement, time and strike, 10" wide, 20" high—$400.

W. Boardman mahogany wall clock, circa 1825, with wooden works, stenciled splat and column case. Tablet is not original, 16-1/2" wide, 31-1/2" high—$300.

Brewster & Ingraham rosewood veneer double OG wall clock, circa 1840, 30-hour, time only, 15" wide, 25-1/2" high—$300.

Label from Birge, Mallory & Co. triple-decker shelf clock. The label reads, "Eight day clocks made and sold by Birge, Mallory & Co., Bristol, Conn. warranted good."

J.C. Brown rosewood steeple clock, time and strike, circa 1850, 10" wide, 19-1/2" high—$400.

L.F. & W.W. Carter rosewood double-dial perpetual-calendar, top dial records days and bottom dial records months and dates, eight-day, time and strike, 13-1/2" wide, 21" high—$600.

E.O. Goodwin rosewood shelf clock, 1852-1855, with gold leaf stenciling on case, eight-day, time and strike, circa 1850s, 9-1/2" wide, 15" high—$800.

Hopkins & Alfred Clock Co. mahogany mirror shelf clock, circa 1825, wooden works, weight-driven, time and strike, 17" wide, 30-1/2" high—$400.

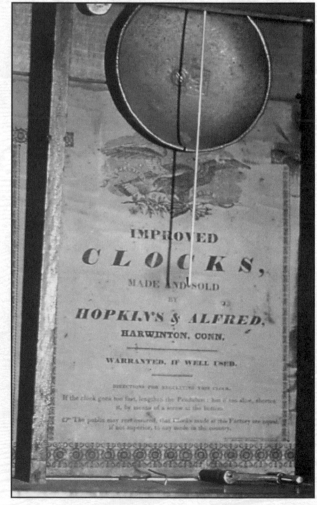

Label from Hopkins & Alfred mirror shelf clock. The label reads, "Improved clocks made and sold by Hopkins & Alfred Clock Co., Harwinton, Conn. Warranted if well used."

Howard Electric clock, circa 1940, time only, Chicago made, 6" wide, 11" high—$150.

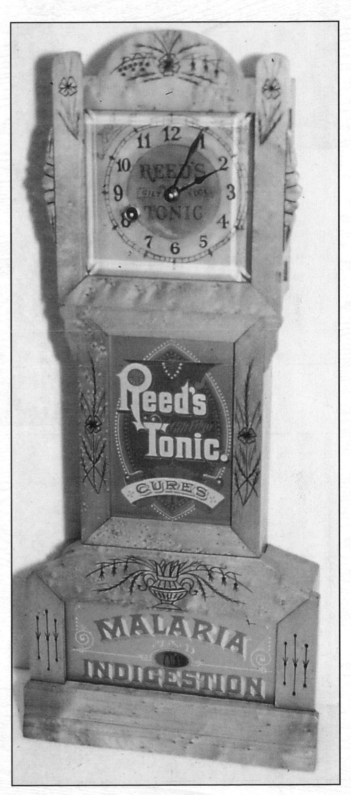

L. Hubel bird's eye maple advertising shelf clock, circa 1870, eight-day, time only, 10-1/2" wide, 24" high—$2,000.

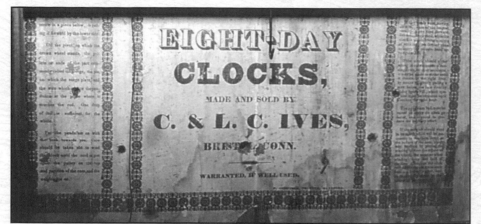

Label from C. & L.C. Ives triple-decker shelf clock. It reads, "Eight day clocks made and sold by C. & L.C. Ives, Bristol, Conn., warranted if well used."

Brass strap movement from C. & L.C. Ives triple-decker shelf clock.

C. & L.C. Ives triple-decker mahogany, circa 1835, shelf clock with side pillars and ball feet, 18" wide, 38" high—$600.

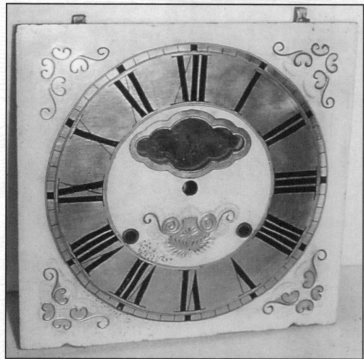

Wooden dial to C. & L.C. Ives triple-decker shelf clock. Notice the opening above the center which allows one to see the movement.

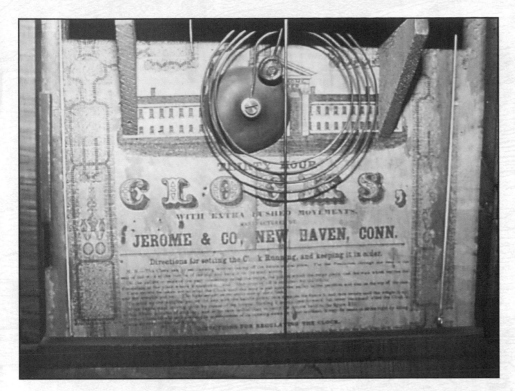

Label from Jerome & Co. transition shelf clock. It reads, in part, "Thirty hour clocks with extra bushed movements, manufactured by Jerome & Co. New Haven, Conn. Instructions for setting the clock running and keeping it in order."

Jerome & Co. rosewood transition shelf clock with half columns, circa 1851, 30-hour, time and strike, weight-driven, 15" wide, 25" high—$250.

Chauncey Jerome rosewood veneer OG mirror wall clock, 30-hour, time and strike, circa 1848, 15" wide, 25-1/2" high—$250.

Label from a Chauncey Jerome OG shelf clock. It reads, in part, "Patent brass clocks manufactured and sold by Chauncey Jerome, New Haven, Conn. warranted good. Directions for setting the clock running and keeping it in order…"

William S. Johnson rosewood
miniature double OG shelf clock,
circa 1860, 30-hour, 12" wide,
18-1/2" high—$200.

View of Seth Thomas eclipse
movement in back of Kroe-
ber china shelf clock.

Lux Clock Company, Inc. miniature celluloid mantle clock, 8" wide, 4-1/2" high—$42.

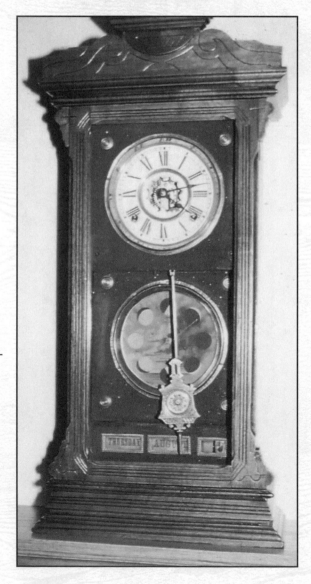

Macomb Calendar Clock Co. walnut perpetual-calendar clock, circa 1882-1883, incised carving, moon phases on lower dial, eight-day, time and strike, 13" wide, 28" high—$4,500.

Elisha Manross mahogany OG shelf clock, 30-hour, time and strike, circa 1848, 15-1/2" wide, 43" high—$300.

Label from Elisha Manross OG shelf clock. It reads, in part, "Patent thirty hour brass clocks made and sold by Elisha Manross, Bristol, Conn. Warranted good. Directions for setting the clock running and keeping it in order."

Label from Manross Prichard & Co. shelf clock. It reads, in part, "Improved brass clocks made and sold by Manross Prichard & Co., Bristol, Conn., warranted good."

Manross Prichard & Co. mahogany OG shelf clock, circa 1850, 16" wide, 26-1/2" high—$350.

Mitchell Vance & Co. iron-front clock with French movement, urn on top, porcelain dial, beveled glass, eight-day, time and strike on a bell, 8-1/4" wide, 16-1/2" high—$400.

Roswell-Kimberly rosewood shelf clock, 1850-1860, with top finials and columns, eight-day, time and strike, 11" wide, 21" high—$500.

Russell and Jones walnut parlor clock, incised carving, eight-day, time, strike and alarm, 14" wide, 22-1/2" high—$250.

Southern Calendar Clock Co., mahogany "Fashion #2," calendar clock, eight-day, time and strike, Pat. July 4, 1876. The cases and the time movements were made by Seth Thomas and the calendar mechanism used was the Andrews Calendar patent. The company was located in St. Louis, MO—$1,400.

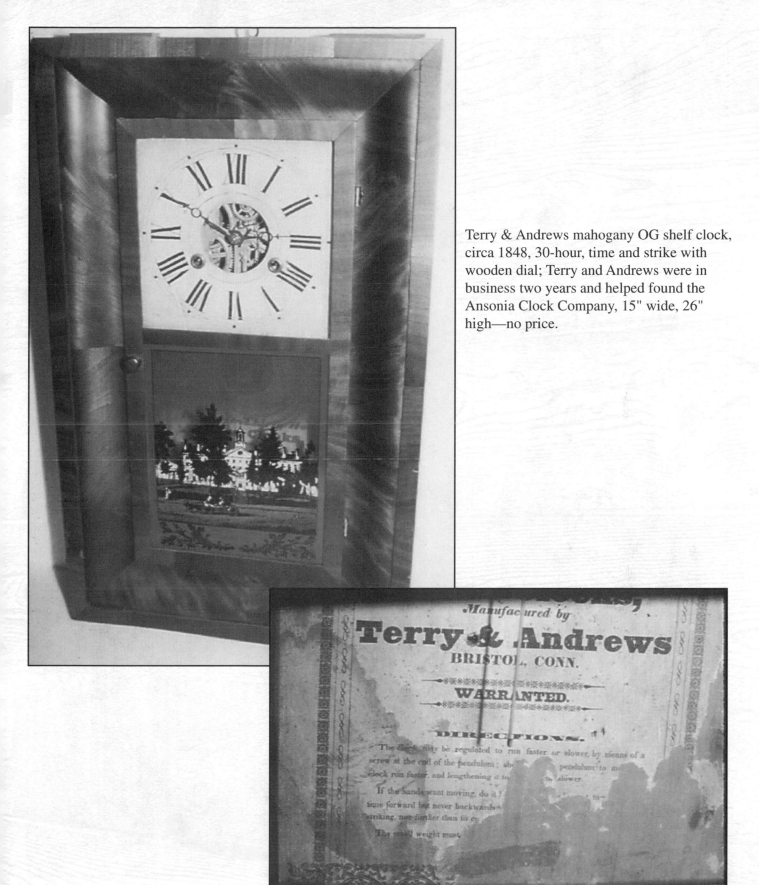

Terry & Andrews mahogany OG shelf clock, circa 1848, 30-hour, time and strike with wooden dial; Terry and Andrews were in business two years and helped found the Ansonia Clock Company, 15" wide, 26" high—no price.

Label of Terry Andrews OG shelf clock. It reads, in part, "Manufactured by Terry & Andrews, Bristol, Conn. Warranted."

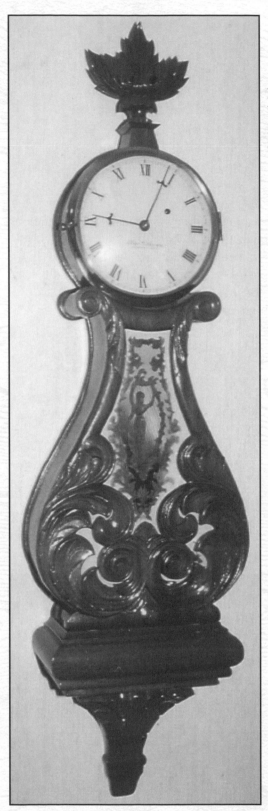

Elmer Stennes mahogany ribbon-stripe banjo clock, marked MCIP (made clock in prison), one weight, time only, 7" dial, 44" high—$2,600.

Welch, Spring & Co. rosewood calendar clock with B.B. Lewis's perpetual movement, patented Dec. 18, 1868, eight-day, time and strike, 11" wide, 20" high—$995.

M. Welton's mahogany, mirror door OG shelf clock, circa 1845, repainted dial. He made both clocks and cases, 30-hour, time and strike, 16" wide, 26" high—$250.

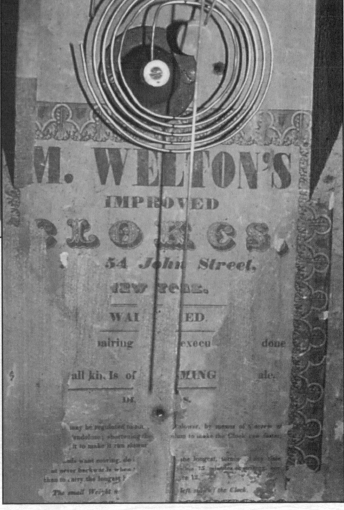

M. Welton label on OG shelf clock. It reads, in part, "M. Welton's improved clocks, 54 John Street, New York. Warranted."

The Western Clock Mfg. Co., La Salle, Illinois, brass-finished iron-front shelf clock with female figure holding up the clock, 30-hour, time only, 6-1/2" wide, 12" high—$145.

Parker of Connecticut iron-front shelf clocks, both with visible escapements. Located on the top of the left clock and on the bottom of the right clock, 30-hour, time only, 6" high—$750 each.

# Chapter 4

# Leading Clock Makers

## Ansonia Clock Company

Anson Phelps, an importer of brass, copper and tin, started the Ansonia Brass Company at Ansonia, Connecticut. In 1850, he founded the Ansonia Clock Company near Derby, Connecticut. Since brass was used for both movements and decorative touches, this helped his brass business as well. From 1851-1878, the Ansonia Brass and Clock Company was also called the Ansonia Clock Company.

After a fire destroyed the factory in 1854, the company relocated at Phelp's Mill. Clockmaking continued under the name of The Ansonia Brass and Copper Company. In 1878, the Ansonia Clock Company was again doing business. Bad luck followed the company's move to Brooklyn, New York, in 1879. A fire soon destroyed the plant. The Ansonia Clock Company reorganized and again manufactured clocks. In 1880, the company opened in Brooklyn.

All sorts of wall and shelf clocks, many with brass embellishments, were produced. Imitation French clocks, as well as novelties, such as the "Bobbing Doll" and "Swinging Doll," patented in 1855 and 1859, respectfully, were marketed. An 1889 catalog showing Ansonia clocks, featured three versions of the Bobbers, called Jumper No.1, Jumper No. 2 and Jumper No. 3. Ansonia was known for its diversity of clock types; many of the older and unusual ones have been reproduced including the previously mentioned "Bobbing" and "Swinging" dolls.

The company's specialty clocks included the Swing Clocks, where female figures held the swinging pendulums. Also popular were the Royal Bonn porcelain shelf varieties and the statue clocks which the company advertised as figure clocks. Among its novelty clocks, the Crystal Palace, Sonnet, Helmsmen and Army and Navy have proved to be excellent collector's items and have rapidly increased in value. The clocks were marked "New York."

After World War I, Ansonia showed steadily increasing financial loses, owing to rapidly decreasing sales, and was forced to abandon its once flourishing clock business. As a result, machinery and some equipment were sold to the Soviet government and were moved to the Soviet Union in 1929.

Ansonia crystal regulator with onyx top and base, visible (or open) escapement, mercurial pendulum, beveled plate glass, porcelain dial, eight-day, half-hour gong strike, 10" wide, 17-1/4" high—$3,400.

## William L. Gilbert Clock Company

In 1828, George Marsh and William L. Gilbert bought a clock shop and formed Marsh, Gilbert & Company. From 1828-1834, they actively pursued their new business in both Bristol and Farmington, Connecticut. However, from 1835-1837, a new associate, John Birge, joined William L. Gilbert. The name became Birge, Gilbert & Company. Empire-style shelf clocks were made.

A change occurred again from 1839-1840 when the Jerome, Grant, Gilbert & Company was formed. It included Chauncey and Noble Jerome and Zelotas Grant. They produced the Jerome inexpensive, brass movement clocks. In 1841, Gilbert and Lucius Clarke bought a clock factory in Winsted, Connecti-

W.L. Gilbert mahogany OG, eight-day, time and strike, weight-driven, 15-1/2" wide, 26" high—$250.

cut. The town was later renamed Winchester. Ezra Baldwin was also connected with the business for a time.

From 1841-1845 inexpensive brass clocks were produced by Clarke, Gilbert & Company. It wasn't until 1845 when the W.L. Gilbert & Company evolved. At this time, Gilbert purchased Clarke's share in the company. Gilbert worked until 1848 when Clarke bought back his share and Gilbert and Clarke were partners again until 1851. A short time later, the name became W.L. Gilbert & Company and remained as such until 1866 when the Gilbert Manufacturing Company was established. Unfortunately, only 30 years after it was purchased, in 1871, the Winsted factory burned down.

William L. Gilbert must have been a strong, stout-hearted man. The ashes of the burned factory must have hardly grown cold when he formed the William L. Gilbert Clock Company that very same destructive year, 1871. That name was retained for 63 years, even though William Lewis Gilbert died in 1890.

From 1880 to about 1900, George B. Owen was the manager and the business expanded under his guidance. From about 1934-1957, there were financial reverses, but the company weathered them and became William L. Gilbert Clock Corporation. The United States was engaged in World Wall II from 1941-1945. Clock production was restricted because metal was necessary for the war effort.

However, the U.S. government permitted the company to manufacture papier-mâché-case alarm clocks, rather than metal ones. After all, the workers had to get to their war-related jobs on time.

General Computing Company took over the company and operated under the name General-Gilbert Corporation. In 1964, the clock division was no longer profitable. It was sold to Spartus Corporation of Louisville, Mississippi and Chicago.

## E. Howard Clock Company

Edward Howard (1813-1904) became an apprentice under the supervision of clockmaker Aaron Willard Jr. David P. Davis was an apprentice there, also, and the two men later formed a partnership that included Luther Stephenson. Until about 1846, the firm name was Stephenson, Howard & Davis, located in Boston.

However, Stephenson soon left the firm. Howard & Davis continued until 1857 when Davis also gave up his partnership in the company. E. Howard & Co., with its factory in Roxbury, Massachusetts, made banjo, regulator and turret clocks, as well as other quality examples including tower clocks. Howard clock prices are high because of their fine quality. Many collectors give them a grade "A" rating.

Among his more expensive and rare clocks, there are regulators which can be priced as high as $20,000. His astronomical clocks, which were made for the principal observatories in the United States, are priceless. The sidewalk or post clocks that were created by the Howard Company are rare and costly.

## The E. Ingraham Company

From 1828-1830, Elias Ingraham, after a 5-year apprenticeship as a cabinetmaker and joiner, designed clock cases for George Mitchell of Bristol, Connecticut. An exotic case he designed had carved mahogany columns, paw feet, turned rosettes and carved baskets of fruit. Ingraham became one of the foremost clock case designers of his time. He was indeed an important man in the clock industry.

From 1830-1833, Chauncey and Lawson C. Ives had Ingraham design cases for their clocks, including an Empire-type, triple-decker style that was made to accommodate a long drop for the weights. Under the name of Ingraham & Bartholomew of Bristol, Connecticut, they set up a cabinet-making shop to produce clock cases. Ingraham sold out to J.C. Brown in 1832.

Using the company's name of Ingraham and Goodrich, Ingraham and Chauncey Goodrich made cases in Bristol from 1832-1840. They owned a shop in Bristol where they manufactured mirrors, chairs and clock cases. In about 1840, they designed a sharp Gothic case that was called a "steeple" clock. It became extremely popular and that type of case is still made today.

From 1841-1844, Ingraham worked in Bristol. Soon Brewster & Ingrahams was formed and it existed from 1844-1852. The members of the firm were the Ingraham Brothers, Elias and Andrew, and Elisha C. Brewster. Between 1852-1855, Elias and his brother, Andrew, worked in Bristol. They used the name E. & A. Ingraham. Ingrahams & Stedman was formed when Andrew sold half of his interest in the firm to Edward C. Stedman.

Unfortunately, the Ingraham factory with all its clock cases, tools and materials, was destroyed by fire in 1855. Many feel that Ingraham's inventive cases were a great contribution to the clock industry.

## Ithaca Calendar Clock Company

In 1865, Henry Bishop Horton (1819-1885) patented a calendar clock with a mechanism that indicated the day, date and month. It featured an automatic correction to accommodate Leap Years. The clock movement, purchased from

E. Ingraham "Nyanza" walnut-stained banjo wall clock, circa 1917, with Ingraham name on dial, eight-day, time and strike, 10" wide, 38" high—$425.

Ithaca Calendar Clock Company walnut perpetual-calendar shelf clock with ebony-applied decorations and turned columns. The dates are pictured in silver around the outer rim of the bottom tablet, and the two rectangular windows show the day and months, eight-day, time and strike, 10" wide, 28" high—$3,000.

other Connecticut dealers, had a special cam to operate the calendar. When the business grew, a new building was erected, but it was destroyed by fire in February 1876. A fine new structure was built and the company was active until about 1918. Calendars were produced in 15 languages and were shipped all over the world. The business began to decline after 1900 and finally went bankrupt.

## F. Kroeber Clock Company

Do you want to own an elite and expensive clock? Buy a Kroeber clock, if you can find one, because they are not readily available. Florence Kroeber was born in Germany in 1840. He was 10 when his family crossed the Atlantic Ocean to settle in New York City. When he was 19, Florence Kroeber became a bookkeeper in the Owen and Clark Clock Store. In 1861, Clark left the company and George B. Owen continued operating the business until he departed to became general manager of the W.L. Gilbert Clock Company in Winsted, Connecticut. Kroeber then acquired the business which marketed both clocks made in the United States and imported ones.

In 1868, Kroeber took in a partner, Nicholas Mueller, also a German immigrant. This arrangement lasted about a year. Mueller opened his own store where he made bronzed cast-metal figurines and figured metal case fronts for clocks. Later Mueller's, daughter became Kroeber's wife.

Kroeber began to design and make clock cases. He ordered movements from Connecticut makers. In 1887,

his successful clock business was incorporated as the F. Kroeber Clock Company and a second store was opened in Manhattan's mid-town area. His 1888 catalog featured more than 250 clocks. Unfortunately, business was poor after a depression hit the country in 1893. Kroeber closed one store and moved into a smaller one. Times were difficult. He filed for bankruptcy in January 1904.

He no longer had a company of his own; for seven years, he worked as a clerk in a clock and watch department of a store. He died May 16, 1911, but his quality clocks remain for others to appreciate. What were his contributions to the industry? Collectors know that his clocks are more costly and harder to find than comparable ones made by the major companies.

It is possible, but not really known with certainly, that Kroeber

F. Kroeber carriage clock, circa 1889, brass case, glass sides and time only, 8" high—$200.

sometimes put his label on mass-produced American and imported clocks. This seems to be a reasonable assumption when a known label reads, "F. Kroeber, agent for the New Haven, Gilbert, Jerome, Atkins, Seth Thomas and other companies." Collectors always examine carefully a clock that is supposed to be a Kroeber. The presence of a Kroeber label, dial or a marked Kroeber movement are especially desirable and can command top prices.

Up until 1899, Kroeber made clock cases in his shop. Two of them resembled Victorian picture frames. Both were patented in 1869. The cast-metal cases Kroeber used came from other companies. Marble and china cases were imported and received American movements. When Kroeber coated cast-iron cases to make them resemble porcelain, he called his patented product, "Porcelene." When Ansonia Clock Company produced clocks with the same porcelain-type finish and colors, Kroeber sued them for infringing on his patent.

Kroeber also developed a patented pendulum that did not have to be removed when a clock was moved. When his business was going well, his catalog contained 200 or more clock models and related items available at his shop. Kroeber appears to have been a hard-working man who maintained his integrity despite his financial difficulties.

If you are interested in dating Kroeber Clocks, the information on the next page (taken from a city directory research) may answer some of your questions relative to the age of a particular clock:

| Name of Company | Address | Date |
| --- | --- | --- |
| F. Kroeber | 25 John St. | 1865-1869 |
| | 10 Cortlandt St. | 1869-1874 |
| | 8 Cortlandt St. | 1874-1882 |
| | 14 Cortlandt St. | 1883-Feb. 1887 |
| | | |
| F. Kroeber Clock Company | 14 Cortlandt St. | Feb. 1887-Dec. 1887 |
| | 360 Broadway | Jan. 1888-1892 |
| | 360 Broadway & 14 Union Square* | 1892-March 1895 |
| | 360 Broadway | March 1895-May 1899 |
| | | |
| F. Kroeber & Company | 14 Maiden Lane | May 1899-Feb. 1904 |
| | | |
| Muller & Kroeber | 25 John St. or 66 Beekman St. | 1868-1869 |

* Clocks may not have been labeled with both addresses, so 360 Broadway may have been used January 1888 through May 1899.

## Lux and Keebler

For 28 years, Paul Lux worked at the Waterbury Clock Company, Waterbury, Connecticut. In 1912, when he sought a change and assisted by his wife and two sons, Fred and Herman, the family embarked on a novel clock project. The four worked together for several years to establish a new company that would make novelty clocks.

All was progressing well when a fire destroyed their efforts. Fortunately, Paul Lux and his wife were not quitters. When their sons marched off to fight in World War I, friends came to their aid. The Lux motto was "Our Clocks Must Go— or We Go." Thus when the two army veteran brothers came home, the Lux Clocks were ready to market.

In 1931, August C. Keebler started the Keebler Company in Chicago. He did not make clocks but had Lux make them for him. The two companies had a reciprocal agreement and marketed the same clocks, but under different names. The Lux and Keebler pendulettes resulted. Current events, people, comic characters, patriotic themes, the Boy Scouts and people ranging from Sally Rand to President Franklin D. Roosevelt were featured on the clocks.

Animated alarm clocks were created. For example, a swinging ball could be seen in a church steeple or a butcher was seen at work chopping meat while a greedy cat watched. A bear danced, while on another clock a monkey climbed as an organ grinder played. A windmill clock could turn. On some clocks there were birds that bobbed. On others cuckoos appeared and disappeared.

In pendulette versions, a black cat could swing his pendulum tail as his eyes moved. Castles, bull dogs, clowns, Rudolf the Red Nose Reindeer, Woody Woodpecker, flowers, a pirate, the Empire State Building, plus many more objects or animals were themes on these pendulettes. These are fun type clocks that cause people to smile. Maybe that's why they are enjoyable to own.

Lux cuckoo pendulette, molded wood, bird sitting on the top, 30-hour, time only, spring-driven, 4" wide, 6-1/2" high—$45.

## New Haven Clock Company

The New Haven Clock Company was organized in 1853. Hiram Camp, Chauncey Jerome's nephew, was the president. The company made inexpensive brass movements for the Jerome Manufacturing Company. In 1855, New Haven purchased the now bankrupt Jerome company. This gave the New Haven Clock Company access to the Jerome facilities in New Haven, Connecticut; thus, the clock company could now make cases as well as movements. Soon, complete clocks were marketed.

Around 1880, the New Haven firm had sales offices in Chicago, England and Japan. It sold its own clocks, as well as those made by Kroeber, E. Howard and Ingraham. It soon became one of the largest clock companies in the United States. Among the clocks produced were French clocks, jewelers' regulators, ebony and mahogany cabinet clocks, wall clocks, including calendar varieties, figure clocks (now called statue clocks) and tall-case hall clocks (affectionately referred to as grandfather clocks).

A novelty, the flying pendulum clock, was patented Oct. 9, 1882, by J.C. Slafter of Minneapolis. The New Haven Clock Company took control of the patent and improved its mechanism and design until it became one of the funniest and most attractive clocks ever produced. Its movement is unique. A flying ball takes the place of the pendulum. It's advertised as the best show-window attraction ever made. This type of clock has been reproduced from time to time.

In 1885, only New Haven clocks, with the exception of a few imported brands, were marketed. In 1910, the company offered a vast variety of clocks; from 1917-1956 the clock maker was a major producer of inexpensive watches. A corporation, The New Haven Clock and Watch Company, took over the company in 1946. Financial woes plagued New Haven from 1956-1959. In 1960, its manufacturing facilities were auctioned off. After 107 years in business, the company no longer existed.

New Haven walnut banjo wall clock, circa 1895, beveled glass with New Haven on dial, time only, 25" high—$185.

## Eli Terry

Near East Windsor, Connecticut, from 1792-1793, Eli Terry Sr. made floor standing clocks that were originally called long-case or tall-case floor clocks Now they are referred to as grandfather clocks. Shorter versions are dubbed grandmother.

Terry was one of the few makers who created several wooden-movement clocks at a time. Water-power driven saws were used. From 1806-1809, he made 4,000 hang-up wooden clock movements, dials, hands and pendulums.

Eli Terry pendulum candlestick novelty clock with china base on wooden frame, 6" diameter, 9" high, time only, original glass dome missing—$250.

To do so, he invented machines to help with this work, including one to cut gear-wheel teeth. Employees Silas Hoadley and Seth Thomas assisted him. The work was done near Warterbury, Connecticut, where more water power was available. In 1810, his two employees bought the plant and Eli moved to Plymouth Hollow, Connecticut.

About 1816, Terry patented a shelf clock with a new outside escapement movement in a pillar and scroll case. Around 1818-1824, Eli Sr., Eli Jr. and Henry became the firm of Eli Terry and Sons of Plymouth, Connecticut. They produced many pillar and scroll clocks with the label "Patent clock invented by Eli Terry made and sold at Plymouth, Connecticut by Eli Terry and Sons." To accommodate the longer fall of the weights, the eight-day triple-decker clock was made 34 to 38 inches high. The 30-hour clock required less height.

Terry clock labels varied constantly and dates on them frequently overlapped. For example, from 1824-1827, Eli and brother Samuel were named on the labels. Then an Eli Terry Jr. label existed from 1824-1830. From 1825-1830, Eli Terry and son, Henry, were located in Plymouth. From 1830-1841, Eli Terry Jr. and Company received mention in Plymouth. The town name was changed to Terrysville in honor of the noted clockmaker, Eli Terry, on Dec. 22, 1831. This meant that Henry Terry, in Terrysville (1831-1837) continued the business he and his father had in Plymouth from 1825-1830. The change in the town's name, from Plymouth to Terrysville, was an honor which could cause a bit of confusion because the Terrysville post office was not established until 1831.

Around 1834, Eli Terry Sr. retired after a financially profitable career. However, he couldn't quite quit as he made some brass movement clocks after his retirement. In the late 1840s, Eli Terry's youngest son, Silas Burnham Terry, formed the S.B. Terry & Company to make clocks.

In 1852, the famous clock maker, Eli Terry, died in the town that changed its name to honor him, but the family story continued. That same year The Terry Clock Company was organized by Silas Burnham Terry and his son in Winsted, Connecticut. Son Silas was the president of the new firm. The company remained in business until 1876. A slight change was made in the town's name after 1872, The "s" was deleted and the name Terryville came into being.

## Seth Thomas

In the early 1800s, Seth Thomas became an apprentice in the cabinetmaker-joiner trade. Around 1808-1810, carpenter Seth Thomas and Silas Hoadley worked under Eli Terry near Waterbury, Connecticut. Eli Terry needed assistance in order to fulfill his contract for 4,000 hang-up wooden clocks, their movements, pendulums, dials and hands. Thomas was the joiner, skilled in wood-working and he also assembled the clocks. He fit the different parts in their proper places so that the clocks were in running condition.

In 1810, Seth Thomas and Silas Hoadley bought Eli Terry's plant. There they made 30-hour clocks with wooden movements and also tall case clocks. In 1813, Seth Thomas sold his share of the business to Silas Hoadley. He then bought a shop in Plymouth Hollow, Connecticut, where he made tall-case clocks with wooden

movements. This became his work place until 1853.

It is said that Seth Thomas paid Eli Terry for the right to make wooden-movement shelf clocks. The label read, "Patent Clocks Eli Terry, Inventor and Patentee, Made and Sold by Seth Thomas, Plymouth, Conn." In 1839, Seth Thomas changed from wooden to 30-hour brass clock movements. In about 1850, he began to use springs instead of weights as clock power.

The Seth Thomas Clock Company operated in Plymouth Hollow from 1853-1865. After Thomas's death in 1859, his sons—Aaron, Edward and Seth Jr.—carried on the business. In 1865, six years after his death, Plymouth Hollow was renamed Thomaston in honor of the Thomas clockmaking family. That same year, Seth

Seth Thomas mahogany flat-top shelf clock, circa 1866 to 1870; (Plymouth Hollow label), Geneva stops to prevent over-winding, eight-day, time and strike, 11-1/2" wide, 15-1/2" high—$200.

Thomas' Sons & Company was formed. It made marine escapement movements for clocks as well as fine pendulum 18-day spring-driven movements.

In 1879, Seth Thomas Sons & Company and the Seth Thomas Clock Company were consolidated. In 1931, the Seth Thomas Clock Company, established in 1853, became a division of General Time Corporation. Seth Thomas's great grandson, Seth E. Thomas Jr., was chairman of the board until his death in 1932. The company's leadership passed out of the hands of the Thomas family and in 1970 became a division of Tally Industries.

## Waterbury Clock Company

In 1850, Benedict & Burnham Manufacturing Company made brass products and became interested in the clock industry. The company went through various name changes. In 1857, the Waterbury Clock Company, Waterbury, Connecticut, was formed as a branch of Benedict & Burnham. The company made a variety of shelf clocks and some tall-case clocks. In 1892, watches were made for Ingersoll. Waterbury also made and sold movements, in addition to their total clocks, including round tops and octagon drop regulators, calendar clocks and various other versions for home use.

In 1922, the company purchased the Robert H. Ingersoll & Brother watch business. In 1944, the company became a part of U.S. Time Corporation.

## E.N. Welch Manufacturing Co.

Before 1831, Elisha Niles Welch was in the foundry business with his father, George. They made clock bells and weights. From 1831-1834, Thomas Barnes and Welch manufactured clocks under the name Barnes & Welch. From 1841-1849, E.N. Welch became a partner of J.C. Brown who used both Forestville Manufacturing Company and J.C. Brown, Bristol, Connecticut, as company names. Chauncey Pomeroy was also a partner. The company made eight-day clocks with brass movements.

Fire destroyed Brown's Forestville plant in 1853. In about 1854, Welch bought Elisha Manross's failing

E.N. Welch mahogany miniature OG, 30-hour, time and strike, original dial and tablet, 12" wide, 19" high—$200.

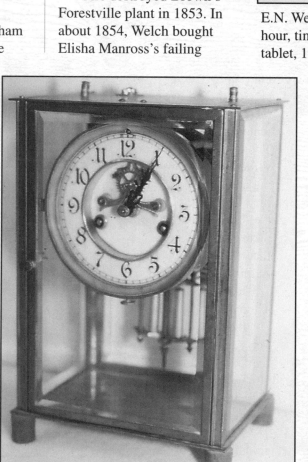

Waterbury polished brass crystal regulator, mercury-type pendulum, open escapement, time and strike, 7" wide, 9-1/2" high—no price.

clock-parts business. In 1856, when J.C. Brown's Forestville Company went bankrupt, Welch purchased it, also. F.N. Otis of Bristol created shelf clocks with fancy pearl inlaid cases. After that company failed, Welch acquired it. These three purchases all occurred around 1856. By 1864, when Welch consolidated his various companies under his name, he owned one of the largest Bristol clock companies.

From 1868-1884, the Welch, Spring and Company partnership in Bristol was formed. Quality regulators and calendar clocks were made. Spring sold his previously purchased Birge, Peck and Company to the new firm. Welch in turn gave the Manross factory to it.

In 1887, Welch died and his son, James, became president of E.N. Welch. Financial problems soon arose. In 1899, the E.N.

Welch movement factory was destroyed by fire; at the end of the year, the case factory burned. In 1902, James Welch died. When the company's financial problems increased, the Sessions family bought stock. In 1903, W.E. Sessions and A.L. Sessions invested money in the company and changed the name to the Sessions Clock Company.

## The Welch, Spring & Company

Three men of different talents—Elisha Niles Welch, Solomon Crosby Spring and Benjamin Bennet Lewis—combined their efforts to make The Welch, Spring

Welch, Spring & Co. "Cary" rosewood parlor clock (named after American contralto, Annie Louise Cary), four decoratively turned columns, Patti movement, eight-day, time and strike, 12-1/4" wide, 20-1/2" high—$1,400.

& Company, an enterprising and successful operation. This union lasted for 16 years, from 1868-1884. What abilities did these three men possess? Welch was the financier, Spring was the manager and design engineer and Lewis was the inventor.

At a time when clocks were being mass-produced and sold in huge numbers at relatively inexpensive prices by the major clock companies in America, for the sake of sales only, these three men devoted their time and effort in the development of a superior, quality clock line.

In 1831, when Welch was 22, he formed a partnership with Thomas Barnes under the Barnes and Welch label. In 1841 and again in 1850, he loaned a substantial amount of money to a fellow clockmaker, J.C. Brown. Welch used his financial skills to purchase Brown's insolvent firm and two other Bristol firms, The Forestville Hardware and Clock Company and the Frederick Otis Case Shop. Feeling the need to consolidate his clock holdings, he formed the E.N. Welch Manufacturing Company. It is easy to see why he was successful. He always seemed to know how to best invest his money. It was Welch, indeed, who gave the financial strength that The Welch, Spring & Co. needed for its success.

Spring gained the majority of his clock experience while he was working for the Atkins Clock Company. He was a case-maker of great

merit, specializing in the rosewood case for which he became well known. After leaving the Atkins Company, he spent about 20 years in business for himself. At 38, he bought the land, buildings and equipment of the Birge, Peck and Company and gave it a new name, S.C. Spring Clock Company. Although he did not make a vast number of clocks in his newly organized company, he did, however, supply cases, movements and parts to other Bristol, Connecticut, clockmakers.

Lewis' contribution to the new company was his astute ability in developing calendar mechanisms. He was issued three patents for perpetual calendar mechanisms on Feb. 4, 1862, June 21, 1864, and Dec. 29, 1868. The clocks that Lewis marketed were labeled either Benjamin B. Lewis or Benjamin B. Lewis and Sons.

During the company's 16 operational years, it went through four stages. The first stage, from 1868-1869, saw the creation of the standard shelf model. Spring concentrated, during this first year, in producing three models—the Empress, the Peerless and the Italian. The next stage concentrated on the production of regulators and calendar clocks from 1870-1876; during this time, the company only made five styles of regulators and five styles of calendars. These clocks were named with numbers from 1 to 5 in both categories giving the buyer 10 choices of either No. 1, 2, 3, 4 or 5 calendars or No. 1, 2, 3, 4 or 5 regulators. All of the calendars used the B.B. Lewis V perpetual calendar mechanism. The cases were walnut or rosewood.

The majority of the No. 1 regulators were made with rosewood cases. The small number, however, that were made with walnut cases have become extremely rare and expensive. They originally sold for $95, a price that would keep them out of most American homes. The four other regulator models specified the type of wood used. In cases 2 and 3, rosewood was used, while in the last two the wood choice was walnut.

The task of creating new model clocks rested on the shoulders of Solomon Spring in the company's third stage from 1877-1888. He needed names which stood for quality and which the general population knew. Other manufacturers were producing clock "series" like the city clocks by Seth Thomas, the architectural names used by Ingraham and the regent and river series by other companies. A decision was made by Spring and staff members that the clock names would be artists from the opera and theater who were known and admired. Therefore, he named his spring models of 1877 after seven artists including the names of Parepa, Lucca, Titiens, Verdi, Kellogg, Auber and Wagner, a combination of composers and sopranos. The variety of styles included were shelf clocks, regulators, shelf and wall calendars and wall octagons. The two shelf clocks in rosewood were the Parepa and the Lucca. The latter also was made as a regulator. The Titiens, a shelf clock, had a walnut case. The octagon wall clock was the Verdi and the Kellogg was a wall regulator in walnut. The other two, the Auber, a shelf calendar, and the Wagner, in both a wall and a shelf calendar, were in black walnut cases.

The Patti Era was the company's fourth and final stage, lasting for five years, from 1879-1884, that marked the company's final effort to stay in business and to remain successful. "As the Patti goes, so goes the company," seemed to sum up the feelings of the Welch, Spring & Company

staff. The original Patti clock had the following characteristics: four fancy column turnings, glass sides, rosettes and fancy finials. The case was rosewood and had a Sandwich glass pendulum. The Patti is considered by many as the most collectible and famous parlor clock ever made by an American manufacturer, but sales were not up to expectations.

Therefore, in order to realize greater sales, the company tried to dress up the Patti. Some of the additions were a brass pendulum with a Sandwich glass center and a gold-leaf border on the door glass. Other changes included black labels with gold print that replaced the white labels with black print, a bell mounted to the movement and French-style cloverleaf hands. The demise of the Welch, Spring and Company came as a result of the expense required to produce these fancy clocks that, in actuality, were too costly to produce and much too expensive for the public to buy. The company ceased business in 1884. All of the buildings, inventory and machinery of the Welch, Spring and Company was purchased by E.N. Welch for $10,000. The mass-production concept had won and the really fancy, expensive clock failed to meet the needs of the average citizen. E.N. Welch, however, died a wealthy man, in 1887, leaving an estate of some $3 million.

# Other Clock Manufacturers

## Joseph Ives

Joseph Ives (1782-1862) of Connecticut was an inventor and a clockmaker. When he entered this trade, wooden clock movements were in use; thus he followed this trend and fashioned wooden movements. Soon, however, he felt brass

ones might be better, especially ones made of rolled-sheet brass. He developed a rolling pinion, a small gear with teeth that fit into those of a larger gear or rack. He also successfully used the wagon or multi-gear spring, which is a series of flat springs instead of a coil one to power a clock movement. In addition, Ives received a patent for a steel spring. He is credited with a possible American-first when he developed a successful clock spring. Up until this time, only England had made the clock spring.

Joseph moved to Brooklyn, New York, in 1826 and made wagon-spring clocks. He headed Joseph Ives & Co., Bristol, Connecticut, from 1818-1819. He was also a prudent advisor for his brothers in other Ives family firms until two years before his death in 1862.

Perhaps the Ives Brothers inherited their interest in clocks from their father, Amasa Ives of Bristol, who worked from the 1770s-1790s. He assigned his own patents to various manufacturers. The six Ives brothers were Ira (1775-1848), Amasa (1777-1817), Philo (1780-1822), Joseph (1782-1862), Shaylor (1785-1840) and Chauncey (1787-1857). One author says these brothers became famous for their part in becoming an integral part of Bristol clock history. This group of men had 11 patents on clocks. Ira received two: one for a time and strike clock and another for pinions. Shaylor earned two for clock springs he developed. Joseph was awarded seven patents. All of the men were a credit to their profession because they all produced quality clocks.

## The Willard Brothers

There were four Willard Brothers who made clocks. They were Benjamin (1743-1803), the third child of 12 siblings, Simon (1753-

1848), the eighth born, Ephram, the ninth born, and Aaron (1757-1844) the tenth.

Benjamin completed his apprenticeship in 1764, and began making clocks in Grafton, Massachusetts. After a time, he opened a shop in Roxbury Street in the Boston area where a colony of artisans lived. There he made a variety of clocks. In 1773, Benjamin ran an advertisement in *The Boston Gazette*. It read, "Benjamin Willard at his shop in Roxbury Street…has on sale musical clocks playing different tunes every day of the week and on Sunday a psalm tune." He further declared that, "The music played once every hour and did not obstruct the clock's motion in any way."

Simon was the second brother to enter the clockmaking trade. He became the most famous of the four siblings. Tall-case clocks (called grandfather's now) were the norm until Simon helped introduce shelf and wall clocks. Around 1800, he began working on an eight-day wall clock. It was patented on Feb. 8, 1802, as his "Improved Timepiece." The pendulum was suspended from the front with the weight at the bottom that allowed the pendulum to be screwed down. This meant the clock could be moved without damaging the suspension. Because of its shape, it was called a banjo clock. The first ones were time only. There was a clear 7-inch dial, fine hands and a mahogany case. The glass was decorated with gold leaf. The weight-driven movement was so accurate that, "It kept well within one minute's error a week." This beautiful instrument won acclaim at once and is still a popular style. Naturally there were others who desired to create similar clocks. They had to make slight changes, however, so as not to infringe on Simon's patent. Simon advertised that he made clocks for church steeples as well as eight-day time pieces. In a 38-year time-span, this man made 4,000 clocks.

Brother Aaron emulated Simon's clockmaking techniques. He made banjo clocks, and the brothers created 30-hour wall time pieces as well. Soon, they and other makers fashioned the earliest known American shelf clocks. Their cases resembled the top portion of a tall case clock. They were called "The Massachusetts Half Clocks."

Ephram, who is not mentioned as frequently as his brothers, appears to have worked for a while in the area where his siblings worked, including Roxbury, Massachusetts, in 1798. However, he left to settle elsewhere. He is listed in New York in 1805. The Willard Brothers did contribute ideas that promoted and expanded the clock industry. Their clocks, with their precise workmanship, were durable and ran well.

# Chapter 5

# Old Timers: Timely Tips

Unknown maker, mahogany shelf clock with stencil top and side columns, wooden movement and dial, 30-hour, time and strike, 32" high—$300.

Only an affluent person could secure the services of a clockmaker in Colonial America of the 1700s. Clocks were hand-crafted, one at a time. The clockmaker customarily melted down the brass in his furnace, cast it, hammered it, turned it and filed it—a long, difficult and tedious process. The total clock from the dial, the hands, the works, to the case was completed in the shop. The clockmaker frequently had apprentices assist him; thus they could learn and gain experience in how to make clocks.

* * *

Originally, in the 1700s, brass founders did the initial preparation of the metal. By 1780, the clock industry was beginning to diversify. Different craftsmen became involved in the clockmaking process. Cast brass parts could be purchased. The clockmakers did the turning, gear cutting, filing and assembly of the clocks.

* * *

Around 1800, wooden movements that were easier to make and cost less than hand-made brass ones, became available.

* * *

In the late 1700s it was possible to purchase paper dials. They came in lots of 24, 28 or 96. These were pasted on wooden panels or iron plates to form the clock faces.

* * *

Early weight-driven clocks were tall because large cases were required to provide an adequate dropping space for the falling weights.

* * *

It was expensive to ship clocks with heavy weights. Because of this, empty sheet-iron cans were included with the clocks. Their new owners could fill these containers with sand or stones to create the weight needed to operate the clock properly.

* * *

When clocks were no longer made-to-order, one by one, clockmakers often became traveling merchants who tried to sell their extra merchandise. At other times, peddlers were employed to sell clocks. Cases frequently were not included because they increased both the weight men had to carry and the cost of the clocks. Therefore, buyers had to use a caseless clock or have a case made.

* * *

Different clock case styles developed after a lot of experimentation by clockmakers. One of the early names that preceded the banjo clock was the coffin clock.

* * *

Edward Howard served as an apprentice to Aaron Willard Jr. and became a prominent and successful maker of clocks. He created the world's first mass-produced watch with the aid of Aaron L. Dennison. Clocks Howard made included banjos, figure-eights, regulators, grandfather's, wall and tower clocks. The Howard-type banjo was first manufactured in 1842 under the name of Howard & Davis. David P. Davis was Howard's partner until 1857. According to some authorities, the finish on the Howard-Davis clocks has never been surpassed.

* * *

An early advertisement for the banjo clock, devised by E. Ingraham Company, listed some of the features for the Treasure Banjo as follows: "an eight-day pendulum movement, equipped with a 2 rod strike, only 39 inches in height, made of genuine mahogany, with an 8 inch etched brass silver plated dial and solid brass side rails." This promotional pitch continued by saying that a more ornate form of the banjo had a lyre shape.

* * *

The Waterbury Clock Company made banjo clocks, eleven of which are shown in their 1908, 1910 and 1917 catalogues. They are all named Willard with a number following, for example Willard No. 4. Two of the eleven are listed as mantel clocks.

* * *

The Waltham Clock Company made reproductions of two early banjo clocks, one of which was the original design of Lemuel Curtis, of Concord, Massachusetts, made between 1810 and 1818. The other is the S. Abbot, Boston, banjo lyre clock. It is over 100 years old.

* * *

Between 1815 and 1818, Lemuel Curtis created the gilted girandole with a round face. It was a variation of Simon Willard's banjo clock. Many consider it to be one of America's most beautiful clocks. Curtis worked in Concord, Massachusetts, from 1814 to 1818, and then in Burlington, Vermont, until 1856.

* * *

In 1816, Eli Terry patented a 30-hour pillar-and-scroll clock. It was America's first mass-produced

shelf clock. Mahogany veneer covered the pine case. The wooden 30-hour movement was driven by two weights. Other makers made a similar clock but varied the case slightly so they would not infringe on Terry's patent. Eli Terry is recognized as the first American to mass-produce low price clocks.

* * *

Eli Terry applied the following labels to his clocks: "E. Terry & Sons, Plymouth," "Eli Terry & Son, Plymouth," "Eli & Samuel Terry, Plymouth," "Samuel Terry, Bristol," "Eli Terry Jun'r, Plymouth." An example of one of his labels reads: "Patent Clock, Made and sold at Plymouth, Conn. by Eli Terry, Inventor and Patentee, Warranted if well used. The public may be assured that this kind of clock will run as long without repairs and be as durable and accurate for keeping time as any kind of common clock whatever."

* * *

The following eight artisans, applying their particular skills, were employed in making patent clocks: the carpenter who made cases, the foundry man who formed the finials, the artist who painted the glass tablet, the goldsmith who made the gold leaf, the die-maker who made the hands, the craftsman who imported and applied the veneers to the cases, the glue-maker who secured the dowels and blocks to keep the case together and the wood carver and the stencil artisan who added embellishments.

* * *

Wooden clock movements in the early 1800s were mostly one-day. When rolled brass became more readily available after 1830, the production of eight-day brass movements increased. However, some wooden movements were still produced.

\* \* \*

Chauncey Jerome (1793-1868) started as a case-maker and influenced the clock trade for 40 years with his designs. He made the bronze looking-glass clock that replaced the pillar and scroll case in popularity. He was the first to use the OG shelf clock case. As a carpenter in 1816, he worked for and made cases for Eli Terry, but soon left to start his own business. He bought clock movements and parts and made the cases for them.

\* \* \*

Chauncey Jerome's brother, Noble, developed a 30-hour weight-driven movement made from rolled brass strips. This was put into an OG case that sold for a low price. The OG was one of America's best selling clocks and maintained its popularity from 1825-1920.

\* \* \*

Women liked the looking-glass clock that Joseph Ives patented in the early 1800s. Instead of a picture or a design, the tablet was a mirror; thus, the clock was both a looking glass and a timekeeper as well. Chauncey Jerome said that it was his idea, but, unfortunately his "bronze looking glass clock" with bronze-colored pilasters, was not patented until about three years after Ive's clock became available. However, Chauncey Jerome's clocks appealed to women in the Southern states. It was reported that New Orleans purchasers paid as much as $115 apiece for them.

\* \* \*

Would you believe that an 1820 census report was included inside a scarce Mark Leavenworth pillar and scroll clock? It was inside the column where the left weight drops. The record shows that New York, the largest state, had a population of 1,352, 812 in that year. In 1818, Illinois became a state. This census said its 1820 population numbered 55,211. Postal rates for 1825 appeared in a corresponding position on the right side of this rare clock. Mark Leavenworth of Waterbury, Connecticut, was in business prior to 1814 and sold wooden uncased movements to other clockmakers. This complete clock of his was marked with his full name as well as the town's name where he worked—Waterbury, Connecticut. (If you wish to see a picture of this clock and its label, it appears on page 29 in the Swedberg's first clock book, *American Clocks and Clock-makers*).

\* \* \*

Shelf clocks with wooden works usually have 30-hour movements. Eight-day examples with this type of movement are uncommon.

\* \* \*

Some clocks from the late 1820s were referred to as transition clocks. These were an in-between style. They were carved or stenciled and often had paw feet. Most had 30-hour weight-driven movements. Frequently, side columns and a stenciled or carved top slat were present. The pillar-and-scroll clock was popular at that time and another, the OG (ogee), was new.

\* \* \*

Double- and triple-deckers followed the transition. They were squatter than the looking glass clocks and often had a splat and side columns. They were either stenciled or carved and had feet.

\* \* \*

A favorite clock from 1825 until 1920 was the OG (ogee) that for a time helped the United States become the world's largest clock-producing country. Another redeeming quality was the part it played in pulling the clock industry out of the 1837 depression. The OG had a box frame that featured the S-curved front door molding and was generally mahogany veneered. A decorated tablet was featured. Early one-day weight-driven examples were about 26 inches high to accommodate the falling weights. The eight-day version usually was taller. When 30-hour spring-driven miniatures appeared, they were 15 or 16 inches tall. The earliest of the OGs, from around 1825 to near 1841, contained 30-hour wooden movements which were replaced by rolled brass movements in the early 1840s. This change followed the lead of Chauncey Jerome who is reputed to have said that he couldn't think of any invention other than the OG clock that has been so useful to so many. Some of the clockmakers and their contributions to the development and improvement of the OG in the early 1800s included:
Silas Hoadley's OG brass works
Terry & Andrews brass weight
C.W. Burnham's 30-hour wood OG
Chauncey Jerome's 30-hour brass
    weight OG
George March's lyre-shaped plates
    from his 30-hour brass movement

\* \* \*

Orton, Preston & Co. mahogany shelf clock, circa 1828-1835, with side columns, wooden movement, 30-hour, single weight, 16-1/2" wide, 31-1/2" high—$395.

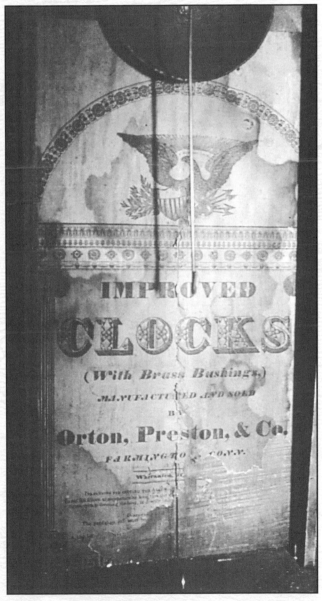

Label from Orton, Preston & Co. shelf clock. It reads, "Improved clocks (with brass bushings) manufactured and sold by Orton, Preston & Co., Farmington, Conn."

Seth Thomas rosewood flat-top shelf clock, side columns, circa 1848, marked Plymouth Hollow, 30-hour, time only, 25" high—$240.

Unknown maker, mahogany shelf clock, wooden dial, side columns, replaced decoration and panels, eight-day, time and strike weight-driven; label in clock gives a partial maker's name as "—ge and Fuller," 17-1/2" wide, 33" high—$250.

Unknown maker, mahogany shelf clock, side columns, time and strike, weight-driven; label in clock names Covington, Indiana, and lists the makers as "Arwood & Cor—"—$250.

C. & L.C. Ives walnut triple-decker
shelf clock, circa 1830, time and strike,
weight-driven, 38" high—$700.

Label from C. & L.C. Ives triple-
decker shelf clock. It reads, "Eight
day clocks made and sold by C. &
L.C. Ives, Bristol, Conn."

Forestville Mfg. Co. (called E.N. Welch, J.C. Brown and C. Pomeroy) mahogany transition wall clock with gilted columns, eight-day, time and strike, weight-driven, 18" wide, 35" high—$400.

Label from Forestville Mfg. Co. transition wall clock. It reads, "Brass clocks. Springs warranted not to fail. Manufactured & sold by Forestville Manufacturing Co., J.C. Brown."

Seth Thomas (Plymouth Hollow) rosewood wall clock, 1850-1863, with cornice and columns, original tablets with reverse painting, eight-day, time and strike, weight-driven, 16-1/2" wide, 32" high—$500.

Label from the Seth Thomas wall clock, Plymouth Hollow, Conn.

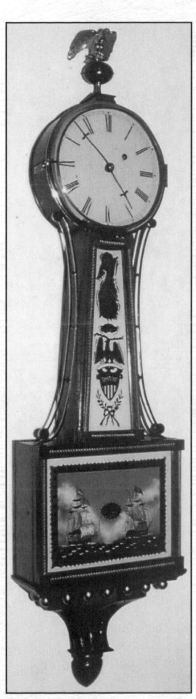

Sessions Clock Company mahog-any-finished banjo wall clock with Sessions on dial, eight-day, time and strike, 6" dial, 10-1/2" wide, 35" high—$265.

Curtis reproduction rosewood banjo wall clock, time only, weight-driven, 10" wide, 42" high—$1,000.

Waltham mahogany banjo wall clock, in the Willard-style, circa 1929, ivory enamel dial, Perry's Victory on glass tablet, weight-driven, 10-1/2" wide, 41" high—$2,000.

Seth Thomas mahogany miniature-mirror round band OG, 30-hour, time, strike and alarm, 11" wide, 16-1/2" high—$170.

Chauncey Jerome mahogany miniature round band OG, circa 1868, eight-day, time, strike and alarm, tablet not original, 11" wide, 16-1/2" high—$350.

Seth Thomas rosewood OG made in Plymouth Hollow, circa 1860, eight-day, time and strike, weight-driven, 15-1/2" wide, 25-1/2" high—$175.

Seth Thomas rosewood miniature, round band OG, circa 1880, 30-hour, time and strike, 10-1/2" wide, 16-1/2" high—$200.

Seth Thomas mahogany OG, eight-day, time and strike, weight-driven, 15" wide, 25" high—$225.

Forestville Mfg. Co. mahogany OG, circa 1855, with maker J.C. Brown on the label, eight-day, time and strike, weight-driven, 16" wide, 29" high—$350.

Seth Thomas rosewood double OG, eight-day, time and strike, weight-driven, 15" wide, 25" high—$300.

Label from Seth Thomas OG shelf clock. It reads, "Eight day weight clocks, Seth Thomas, Thomaston, Conn., Warranted good."

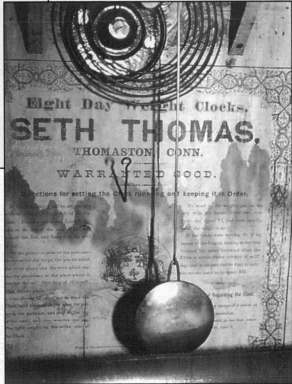

Seth Thomas rosewood round band OG, circa 1885, eight-day, time and strike, weight-driven, 15" wide, 25" high—$300.

E.N. Welch rosewood OG, circa 1875, 30-hour, time and strike, 15" wide, 26" high—$300.

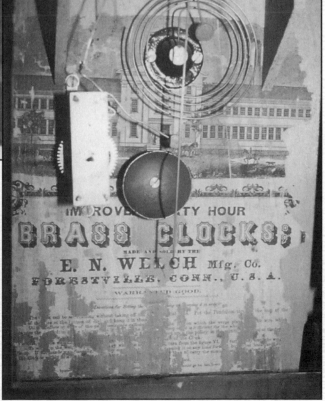

Label from E.N. Welch OG shelf clock. It reads, "Improved 30-hour brass clocks made and sold by E.N. Welch Mfg. Co., Forestville, Conn., warranted good."

Elisha Manross mahogany double OG, circa 1845, 30-hour, time and strike, 15-1/2" wide, 26" high—$250.

Label from Elisha Manross OG shelf clock. It reads, "Thirty hour clocks warranted good. Made and sold by Elisha Manross, Bristol, Conn."

Chauncey Jerome mahogany OG, circa 1845, replaced picture on tablet, 15-1/2" wide, 26" high—$300.

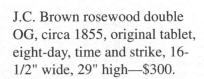

J.C. Brown rosewood double OG, circa 1855, original tablet, eight-day, time and strike, 16-1/2" wide, 29" high—$300.

J.C. Brown rosewood oversized OG, circa 1855, eight-day, time, strike and alarm, 16-1/2" wide, 31" high—$300.

J.C. Brown rosewood wall hanging OG, 30-hours time and strike, reverse painting on tablet, 15-1/2" wide, 25-1/2" high—$250.

# Chapter 6
# Classic Clocks: Timely Tips

The works for Germany's Royal Bonn porcelain clocks were usually made in the United States, many of them by the Ansonia Clock Company. The clocks were decorated in rich colors—green, ruby, turquoise or violet. Cobalt blue was also available. Other features on these clocks included a French or rococo sash, beveled glass, porcelain visible escapement with a choice of an Arabic or a Roman dial.

* * *

A Royal Bonn Clock should be marked as such in order to be identified positively. German Dresden clock cases must be labeled also. They frequently had American-made movements.

* * *

A crystal clock has glass panels on four sides which exposes the works to full view.

* * *

Ormolu had its origin in France in the 17th century. It is fancy metal-work made from gilded cast bronze that was used for decorating clock cases. By the early 18th century. almost the entire cases were embellished with ormolu.

* * *

A porcelain clock displayed in this chapter is marked Royal Bonn. Its movement has the Ansonia mark.

* * *

A catalog description of porcelain clocks list some of the following phrases: assorted decorations, raised decorated flowers, Wedgewood decorations, rich color decorations, hand-painted decorations, floral designs, richly decorated and tinted cases.

* * *

Among the Waterbury Clock Company's crystal regulator clocks, the one named "Paris" seems to be the most elaborate and expensive. It sold for $50 in the early 1900s. Waterbury finishes are varied to include one of the following—rich gold plated, Syrian bronze, polished brass and polished mahogany. Other characteristics include ivory dial and center, visible or open escapement, beveled-glass front, sides and back, and a cast gilt bezel.

* * *

New Haven figure clocks have a common feature, in that a clock and a figure (sometimes, but not often, there are two) rest on a base which has been finished in gilt or bronze. The Ansonia statue clocks have a design similar to those made by New Haven. Their bases are finished in either Syrian bronze, Barbedienne bronze or Japanese bronze.

* * *

In 1902, W.L. Gilbert made a crystal regulator, named "Verdi," that was an eight-day, half-hour strike. It had an ivory dial, visible escapement, mercurial pendulum and front, sides and back beveled glass. It was finished in a rich, ormolu gold. Its original cost was $60.

* * *

A 1910 W.L. Gilbert catalogue shows a crystal regulator clock called "Magdeleine." The case is made of rich Brazilian onyx with round tapering onyx columns. The mountings are gold-plate with heavy ornamental case decorations in rich ormolu gold plate finish. It

was listed at $100 in the catalog. There was a lion top ornament available for an additional $3.

* * *

The Boston Clock Company, in its 1890 catalog, had a clock named "Alhambra," with a Damaskeen finish. It had a gold-plated case and an all-jeweled movement. The front, back and sides were of beveled glass.

* * *

One of the most expensive crystal regulators put out by the Ansonia Clock Company was the Regal clock listed in its 1906 catalog. It was finished in rich gold or Syrian Bronze. It had an eight-day, half-hour gong striking movement, porcelain dial, visible escapement and beveled plate glass all around. Today this clock sells for well over $2,000.

* * *

Ansonia came out with a series of six cabinet clocks, called Cabinet A, Cabinet D, Cabinet F, Senator, Cabinet Antique and Cabinet No. 1. They were made of antique oak, mahogany, polished mahogany or polished oak with brass trimmings. They ranged from 19 inches to 23 inches high. Today, the Senator is probably the most valuable, selling for in excess of $1,500.

* * *

Among the Seth Thomas Empire line are two unique crystal regulators called Empire No. 31 and Empire No. 32. Each has a bronze-finished girl's head on top of the clock. These are among the most expensive in this line.

French brass crystal regulator with mercury pendulum, porcelain hand-painted face, convex glass with beveled edges, time and strike on a coil gong, 7" wide, 10-1/2" high—$800.

French Le Coultre brass crystal regulator, open escapement, 15 jewels Atmos perpetual-motion clock, 8-1/2" wide, 9" high—$775.

German polished brass crystal regulator, circa 1878, single mercury vial, time only, 8-1/2" high—$425.

Ansonia "Regal" crystal regulator, finished in rich gold, visible (or open) escapement, mercury pendulum, beveled glass, eight-day, half-hour gong strike, 10-1/2" wide, 18-1/2" high—$3,400.

Boston Clock Co. "Alhambra" crystal regulator, patented Dec. 20, 1880, beveled glass, gold-plated case, 11-jeweled movement, porcelain dial, tandem wind movement, eight-day, time strike. New cost was $133. It is 14" wide, 23-1/2" high—$3,000.

Ansonia "Apex" crystal regulator, finished in rich gold, porcelain dial, open escapement, beveled glass, eight-day, time and strike, 10" wide, 19" high—$2,800.

Ansonia "Admiral" polished mahogany crystal regulator, finished in rich gold, porcelain dial, mercury pendulum, open escapement, beveled glass, eight-day, time and half-hour gong strike, 10" wide, 18" high—$3,400.

Ansonia Royal Bonn porcelain shelf clock with open escapement, porcelain dial, eight-day, time and strike, 13-1/2" wide, 15" high—$800.

Austrian porcelain shelf clock, circa 1890, 30-hour, time only, 6-1/2" wide, 7" high—$100.

Ansonia porcelain shelf clock with German case, eight-day, time and strike, 9-1/2" wide, 9" high—$400.

Ansonia "La Charny" Royal Bonn porcelain shelf clock, porcelain dial, French sash bezel, eight-day, time and strike, 11" wide, 12" high—$450.

Two marks on the back of the Ansonia "La Charny" are "Royal Bonn" and "Ansonia Clock Company, New York."

Ansonia "La Orne" Royal Bonn porcelain shelf clock, circa 1890, porcelain dial, eight-day, time and strike, 12" wide, 11" high—$575.

Ansonia "La Clair" Royal Bonn porcelain shelf clock, porcelain dial, rococo sash on door, circa 1890, eight-day, time and strike, 9-1/2" wide, 13" high—$550.

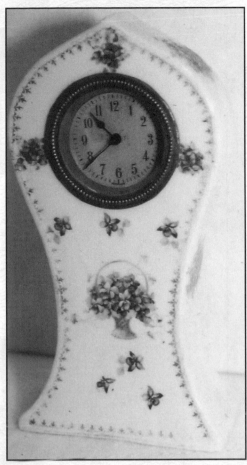

German-made porcelain shelf clock with brass trim around dial, time only, 4" wide, 20" high—$125.

New Haven porcelain shelf clocks with blue and white delft colors, 7-1/2" to 10" height range— $250 each.

New Haven "Thistle" porcelain hanging wall clock, with brass surround and wall chain, 15-day, time only 10" wide, 14" high—$600.

New Haven porcelain hanging wall clock, patented July 1895, secondhand, eight-day, time only, 7" diameter—$300.

Porcelain shelf clocks: left, Ansonia showing baby with clock; middle, German-made colored green and white; right, New Haven, colored green and white, circa 1900, 6" to 8" height range—$250 each.

Ansonia "Pizarro" statue clock, original Japanese bronze finish, porcelain dial, visible escapement, beveled glass, rococo sash, eight-day, time and strike, 19-1/2" wide, 21-1/2" high—$1,600.

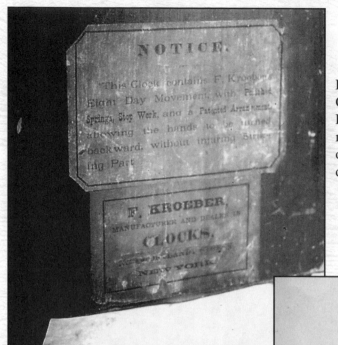

Label from F. Kroeber's statue clock reading, "This Clock contains F. Kroeber's Eight Day Movement with Polished Springs, Stop Work, and a Patented Arrangement allowing the hands to be turned backward, without injuring Striking Part. F. Kroeber, manufacturer and dealer in clocks."

F. Kroeber statue clock of a bowman on top of the metal clock which contains Kroeber's eight-day movement and a patented arrangement allowing the hands to be turned backwards without harm, eight-day, time and strike, 15" wide, 23" high—$700.

Seth Thomas & Sons "No. 8028" statue clock with work by Mitchell, Vance & Co. of a lady sitting on a throne playing a harp, circa 1880 to 1890, eight-day, time and strike, 14" wide, 18" high—$1,000.

Ansonia "Arcadia" swing statue or figural clock, factory-finished in bronze and nickel, originally made for jewelry store windows as attention-getters, eight-day, time only, 4-1/2" dial, 31-1/2" high—$4,500.

Ansonia "Fortuna" swing statue or figural clock, original bronze finish with gilt pendulum, eight-day, time, 4-1/2" dial, 30" high—$4,500.

Ansonia "Gloria" swing statue or figural clock, barbedienne bronze finish, gold numbers on dial and gilted pendulum, eight-day, time, 4-1/2" wide, 28-1/2" high—$3,800.

Ansonia "Juno" swing statue or figural clock, bronze finish, gilted pendulum, eight-day, time, 4-1/2" dial, 28" high—$3,500.

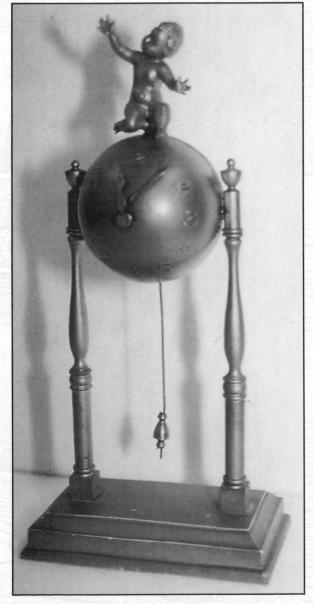

European statue novelty clock of a boy on top of the world, brass finish, 5" wide, 11" high—$175.

Ansonia "Undine and Gloria" statue clock of girl with harp and wings. "Undine" is the name of the base and "Gloria" is the statue's name. Has a porcelain dial, original finish, eight-day, time and strike, 16" wide, 28" high—$1,800.

Ansonia "Olympia" statue clock, bronze finish, beveled glass, porcelain dial, balance wheel escapement, eight-day, time and strike, 15-1/2" wide, 24-1/2" high—$1,500.

Ansonia "Florida Group" statue clock of two girls with bird and flowers, open escapement, chartreuse dial, ormolu trimmings, eight-day, time and strike, 12" wide, 36" high—$3,800.

New Haven statue clock of standing cupid figure, bronze and brass, 4-1/2" wide, 6-1/2" high—$135.

Ansonia "Sibyl & Winter" statue clock, with two cupids on base, original finish, eight-day, time and strike, 16-3/4" wide, 27" high—$1,500.

Seth Thomas "The Whistler," gilt-finished statue clock, eight-day, time, 14" high—$500.

F. Kroeber "Noiseless Rotary No. 2," statue clock of a woman with a parasol sitting on top of a black-enameled mantel clock. Patented June 18, 1878, when Kroeber was located at No. 14 Cortlandt Street (Old Number 8) New York, eight-day, time and strike, 9-1/2" wide, 22" high—$1,500.

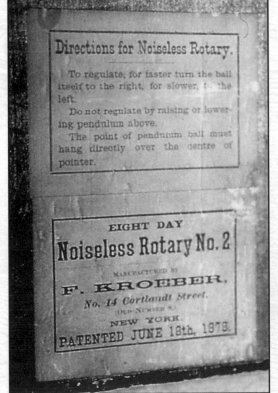

Label from F. Kroeber Eight Day Noiseless Rotary No. 2. Directions for Noiseless Rotary: "To regulate, for faster turn the ball itself to the right, for slower, to the left. Do not regulate by raising or lowering pendulum above. The point of pendulum ball must hang directly over the centre of pointer. Eight day, noiseless rotary No. 2 manufactured by F. Kroeber, No. 14 Cortlandt Street (old number 8) New York, patented June 18, 1878."

W.L. Gilbert statue clock, porcelain dial, metal and bronze clock and bronze figure at side with marbleized wooden base and cast feet, circa 1900, eight-day movement, 14-1/2" wide, 14" high—$400.

New Haven statue clock with cupid, gilted metal, 30-hour, time only, 5" wide, 6-1/2" high—$350.

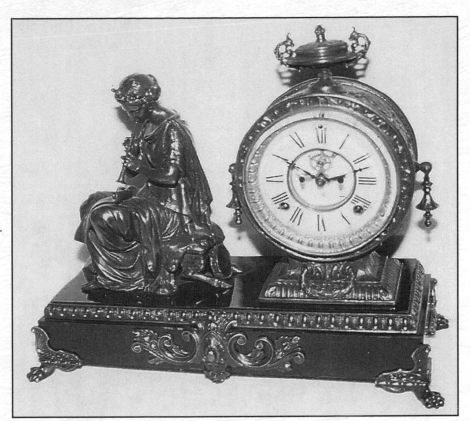

Ansonia "Fantasy" statue clock, circa 1890, porcelain dial, open escapement, bronze finish, French rococo sash, eight-day, time and strike, 17-1/2" wide, 14" high—$600.

Ansonia "Hermes" statue clock, circa 1895, porcelain dial, eight-day, time and strike, 16" wide, 15" high. On the original clocks, the buyer had a choice of three different finishes, named Japanese Bronze, Syrian Bronze or Barbedienne—$650.

Ansonia "Shakespeare" statue clock, porcelain dial, open escapement, bronze finish, French rococo sash, beveled glass, eight-day, time and strike, half-hour gong, 17-1/2" wide, 15" high—$650.

Waterbury and Canadian boudoir metal statue clocks, gilted finish, time only; left, Waterbury with buffalo; center, Canadian with child holding the clock; right, Waterbury; 5-1/2" to 9" height range—$150 each.

French statue clock, circa 1880, finished with brass and porcelain inserts, classical-style, eight-day movement by Japy Freres, 16-1/2" wide, 12-1/2" high—$2,225.

Ansonia novelty statue clock with croquet players, brass and porcelain dial, French rococo sash, patented April 28, 1876, time only, 8" wide, 7-1/2" high—$250.

Warner cupid iron-front statue clock, dated May 15, 1906, porcelain face, bronze finish with cupid holding up the clock, time only, 6" wide, 9-1/2" high—$135.

W.L. Gilbert "Beatrice" with harp statue clock with bronze finish, mercury pendulum, open escapement, French rococo sash, eight-day, time and strike, 13" high—$1,000.

Unknown maker, Spanish American War iron-front statue clock with bronze finish, time only, 10" wide, 11" high—$235.

W.L. Gilbert "Mignon" statue clock, shown in their 1900 trade catalogue, gilt-finished case, statue and feet, porcelain dial, nickel-plate movement, marbleized base, all original, seven-day time and strike—$545.

Ansonia "Summer and Winter" statue clock with a bronze finish, porcelain dial, open escapement, French rococo sash, beveled glass, eight-day, time and strike with half-hour gong, 24" wide, 22" high—$3,000.

Unknown maker, "Father Time" American brass-finished statue clock, wall mounted, patented Sept, 22, 1885, time only, 10" wide, 11" high—$250.

# Chapter 7

# Shelf Clocks: Timely Tips

Shelf clocks were meant to stand on a table, shelf or mantel. This type of clock became popular because it could be produced more easily and economically than the tall case clocks.

\* \* \*

During the last quarter of the 19th century, four forms of shelf clocks took over the market. Walnut creations prevailed from around 1870 to 1900; blacks were in favor from 1880 to just before 1920; oaks achieved their popularity from 1890 until well into the 1900s; and alarms were in vogue from 1875 adinfinitum.

\* \* \*

A cottage clock, first made around 1875, is a smaller form of the Connecticut shelf clock. Most examples have 30-hour movements, wooden cases that are normally less than one foot in height with tops that were either flat or three-sided. The majority were made in the last quarter of the 19th century.

\* \* \*

Elias Ingraham of Bristol, Connecticut, received the credit for designing the steeple clock with its pointed Gothic feel. The clocks could have two or four steeples. They were produced around 1840 when brass-coiled springs were available. Steeple clocks are still made today. The heights of these clocks range from 10-1/2" to 24" with the two in-between sizes of 14-3/4" and 20".

\* \* \*

The bracket clock is not, in reality, a mantel clock because it stands on a decorative, matching bracket attached to the wall.

\* \* \*

A beehive, a Connecticut shelf clock, has a rounded Gothic arch that resembles the inverted hull of a ship. Its average dimensions were 18-1/2" high and 11" wide. Since it was popular, it was produced from the late 1840s until the early 1900s by most major clockmakers.

\* \* \*

Papier-mâché shelf clocks were manufactured in the middle 1800s. Originally, it was a mashed paper, mixed with glue and other adhesive materials, that could be molded. Sometimes, mother-of-pearl and its imitations were added as decoration. Credited with being the largest producer of this type of clock is the Litchfield Manufacturing Co., of Litchfield, Connecticut. Another firm known to have made these cases was the Otis & Upson Co., of Marion, Connecticut. Later, "iron mâché" developed. It was a painted and gilted process applied to cast-iron fronts in an attempt to imitate real papier-mâché.

\* \* \*

Throughout the 1850s, hundreds of different stencil patterns were available for decorating clock tablets. Etched glass examples appeared after 1840. By the late 1800s, clock tablets with decalcomania (decals) transfers were common. They were not, however, considered as desirable as the earlier reversed-painted ones.

\* \* \*

The tambour clock, also referred to as a "camelback" or a "hunchback," was a shelf clock with a rounded top. This style was introduced at the beginning of the 20th century and is still being produced.

\* \* \*

Seth Thomas died in 1859, but his family continued the business.

In the 1880s, bronze statues were made and sold to other manufacturers. They were used to replace missing or damaged ones on old clocks. Today, some companies produce these reproduction figures. It's also possible to purchase hands, dials and finials. Collectors sometimes replace dials, but the originals are kept so the clocks are authentic. If a collector is a purist, he or she does not make additions or changes. The clocks are kept in as near their original condition as possible.

\* \* \*

In 1889, the Ansonia Clock Company offered a group of three oak shelf clocks for a special price of $12.60. Their names were the "Gallatin," "Echo," and "Griswold." They were eight-day clocks with gong strikes. Ansonia claimed they were "Sure Sellers" and potentially "Big Money Makers."

\* \* \*

The Ansonia Clock Company presented an exciting offer when it advertised its 1893 clock special. The ad encouraged buyers by saying, "Our New Bankers Clock Assortment" with all six clocks available for $12.50. The names of the three with walnut cases are "Berkeley," "Buffalo," and "Beaver." The three oak clocks listed were "Belmont," "Bedford," and "Burton." All of these clocks were eight-day strike clocks, 22-1/2" high with 6" dials. The two that had alarms were the walnut Beaver and the oak Burton. The shipping case was provided free, but a customer had to take all six clocks. Imagine what this assortment would sell for today.

\* \* \*

Seth Thomas produced a series of "City" clocks which were named after American and international cities. The clocks were all eight-day, time and strike, spring-driven and were available with a choice of walnut, rosewood or oak cases. Some of the international cities were Athens, Cambridge, Oxford and Rome. Twelve or more others were named after U.S. cities.

* * *

A clock series, circa 1880, named after world rivers was done by the New Haven Clock Company. They were mantel, eight-day, time and strike clocks with walnut cases. Some names were Rhine, Thames, Seine, Volga, Tiber and Danube.

* * *

W.L. Gilbert came out with a series of fish and animal clocks around 1891. Both sets had eight-day movements and were finished in either walnut or oak. The fish—bass, carp, pike, salmon, shark and trout—had an average height of 22 inches, whereas the animals—buffalo, hyena, leopard, lion, panther and tiger—were slightly smaller with a height or 21 inches.

* * *

Marbleized or black mantel clocks became popular around 1880 as a result of the shortage of black walnut which had been used extensively for clock cases. The black marble-top finish can be kept clean and attractive by the use of sweet oil, a suggestion found in an early century Sears catalogue.

* * *

Many clocks were styled in black marble and onyx which were elaborately engraved and inlaid. Brass ornamentation added to their character. Soon, the black marble was imitated with the use of enameled cast iron. The three kinds of material used in the production of these "blacks" were marble, black iron and black-enameled wood.

* * *

Mantel clock assortments were being offered at reasonable prices. A special carload buy of six highly embossed oak cases with E. Ingraham movements was listed at $8.20. An advertisement read, "Our imitation French marble clocks are a reproduction of the French designs in wood, HIGHLY POLISHED, nicely engraved and gilted. We guarantee the finish on these cases to stand equal to any iron case on the market."

* * *

On the B.B. Lewis' Perpetual Calendar label (patented Feb. 4, 1862) a warning to the owner reads, "Never open this door between the hours of 8, P.M., and 8, A.M., as the Bar which moves the Calendar is in the way of the Pin between these hours."

* * *

The Welch, Spring and Company named clocks after female soprano opera stars. One star that was used both in their clock styles and their movements was Adelina Patti, a native of Spain. She was the prima donna of the opera scene, but quite arrogant with fits of temper. The company used Patti in their clock names, calling one variety Patti V.P., and another Patti No. 2 V.P. The V.P. stood for visible pendulum. The company hoped to capture more of the market by dressing up the Patti with the following additions: a highly ornamental brass pendulum bob with a sandwich glass center, a gold-leaf border added to the door glass, a black label with gold print, a bell mounted to the movement and black-flocked paper on the inside of the backboard. The Patti label had either one or two of Solomon C. Spring's patent dates (March 25, 1879 and/or May 20, 1879). The smaller Patti had 6" columns whereas the larger Patti had 12" columns. When the Patti appeared in 1880, two other models also were introduced, named The

Cary V.P. and the Gerster V.P. Although these two clocks did not achieve the popularity of the Patti, her name was used to describe them. The Gerster was referred to as the Patti with the fence around the top and the Cary was the Patti with the little sausages on the top.

* * *

The pressed design on many of the oak shelf clocks was created by a rotary press that forced the design into the wood which had been previously softened with steam. Oak shelf clocks, commonly called kitchen clocks, maintained their popularity from the late 1800s to around 1915.

* * *

The oak or kitchen clock was produced in large numbers by the larger clock companies with perhaps Ingraham being the largest producer. Heights were about 23" with substantial eight-day long-wearing striking movements. The designs were produced by those who made mold and embossing dyes. Many had figures, such as Admiral Dewey (Ingraham and Welch), President McKinley (Ingraham) and Admiral Schley (Welch) on the middle top front of the clock.

* * *

Seth Thomas had the exclusive right to use the Adamantine finish. This gave wooden clocks a marble look. These black-case clocks were often called blacks. Major clock catalogs featured the black-enamel wood clocks and described them as "Finished to imitate black Italian marble and green Mexican onyx." In a trade catalog by E. Ingraham Co., it was stated, "Our imitation French marble clocks are a reproduction of the French designs in wood, HIGHLY POLISHED, nicely engraved and gilted. We guarantee the finish of these cases to stand equal to any iron case on the market."

* * *

During the heyday of clock-manufacturing, skilled mechanics earned about $3 for a 10-hour day. On the other hand, a common laborer made only $1.50 for his efforts.

* * *

The early plastic Celluloid was patented in 1869.

* * *

One of the first marine movement makers in America was Samuel Emerson Root who worked in Bristol, Connecticut, in the 1850s. Although Root did not ordinarily make clocks, an example of an iron-front wall clock with his signature is found on page 97 in the Swedberg's book, *American Clocks and Clockmakers*. Because the case of the clock was made by Nicolas Muller in his New York City foundry, Root must have made the clock's works. Nicolas Muller's Sons produced bronze shelf clocks, also.

* * *

Round alarm clocks, a shape that is universally associated with this type of clock, have been made since the 1880s. The Western Clock Manufacturing Company was established in La Salle, Illinois in 1895. It marketed the Big Ben in 1910 and Little Ben in 1915. Today, they are produced by Westclox, which became the company name in 1936.

* * *

The earliest mechanical clocks were alarm clocks that were used in monasteries by the monks to keep their appointments. These alarms were without dials and simply sounded a bell to awaken the monk.

* * *

"Higher Sprier" and "Lower Slower" is a good way to remember that raising the bob on a pendulum rod shortens the pendulum's swing so the clock goes faster. Lowering it makes the arch wider and slows the clock's speed.

* * *

Ansonia produced a series of

Swing Clocks, between 23" to 31" high, during the last part of the 1800s and the first part of the 1900s. Some of the names were Fisherman Swing, Fisher & Falconer Swing, Diana Swing, Huntress Swing, Gloria Ball Swing and Fortuna Ball Swing. The clocks are finished in Art Nouveau and Syrian Bronze. The balls, which featured the clocks' faces, were enameled in red or blue.

* * *

An agreement sometime in the 1870s between the Seth Thomas Clock Company the Culver Brothers of St. Louis, resulted in the establishment of a sales center in St. Louis called The Southern Calendar Clock Company. Here a double-dial calendar clock with the word "Fashion" on the tablet was marketed. It used the Seth Thomas time movements and its Andrews calendar mechanisms. Their success was minimal; in 1889, their business failed.

* * *

Left, Ansonia flower girl alarm clock, 7" high—$350; right, Ansonia cupid alarm clock, 6-1/2" high—$350.

Left, Ansonia "Snap" alarm clock with dog beneath clock, 8-3/4" high—$400; right, Ansonia "Pride" alarm clock, circa 1880, with figures flanking clock, 7-1/2" high—$400.

Three alarm clocks: left, advertises Quincy, patented 1907, dual alarm—$65; middle, New Haven Intermittent—$70; right, National Call, eight-day, alarm, radium dial that glows in the dark—$85.

Two alarm clocks: left, an Echo, patented Mar. 27, 1877, whose hand moves automatically and rings bell, 7-1/2" high—$1,500; right, grandfather's moon dial like the big ones, 6" high—$1,200.

English alarm, circa 1870, 3-1/2" dial with brass ball pendulum and eight-day, time—$90.

Close-up view of English alarm and its ball pendulum.

Three alarms: left, Pauls Jewelry Co., Burlington, Iowa; middle, Jordan Jeweler & Optician, Davenport, Iowa; right, Big Ben advertising C. G. Samuelson Jeweler, Orion, Illinois—$75 each.

Two alarms; left, double bell Snoopy, 3-1/2" diameter—$25; right, novelty clock showing Amos and Andy with Kingfish, 5" diameter—$50.

French carriage alarm clock with carrying handle, time only, 4" diameter—$500.

Three alarms; left, advertises Muscatine, Iowa's radio station K-TNT—$50; middle, Big Ben eight-day alarm advertising Geo. H. Alps, Jeweler & House Furnisher, Burlington, Iowa—$65; right, chicken on the dial that advertises Cruso H.S.B. & Co.—$50.

Three alarm clocks: left, Ansonia "Amazon," 5" dial; middle, Ansonia, 5" dial; right, New Haven Giant, 5" dial—$150 each.

Two alarms; left, advertises McCabe Jewelers, Rock Island, Illinois—$70; right, advertises Frank the Jeweler, Muscatine, Iowa—$60.

Toulouse-Lautrec French novelty alarm clock; when alarm goes off the hand moves down, lights a match on the striker at base and goes back up to light the candle in the top, 5-1/2" wide, 10" high—$800.

Ansonia simple calendar shelf clock, eight-day, 8-1/2" high—$250.

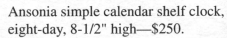

French carriage-style perpetual-calendar shelf clock, brass case, open escapement, small dials for alarm, day, date and month, time and strike, 4-1/2" wide, 8" high—$4,200.

Unknown maker, mahogany simple calendar shelf clock, time only, eight-day pendulum movement, 10" wide, 17" high—$700.

Two Ansonia ink-well calendar shelf clocks; left, "Lily," 30-hour, simple calendar, 7" high—$600; right, "Gem," 30-hour, perpetual-calendar, 7-1/2" high; this latter clock did not sell well because the numbers were too small to read at a distance—$750.

New Haven oak perpetual-calendar shelf clock, with two parallel dials, inscribed lines, eight-day, time only, 14" wide, 13" high—$1,800.

German black ebony-painted case, perpetual-calendar shelf clock with the day, date and month information in the window at the base of the clock, eight-day, time and strike, 12" wide, 19" high—$700.

F. Kroeber oak "Summit" centrifugal calendar shelf clock, circa 1877, eight-day, time and strike, 21-1/2" high—$600.

Close-up of F. Kroeber's calendar shelf clock dial which has dates encircling inner rim and "Calendar Patented July 1877" at the top of the inner circle.

Ithaca Calendar Clock Company, "The Emerald" walnut perpetual-calendar shelf clock with ebony trim. Provisions for the date, day and month are on the lower round tablet, eight-day, time and strike, 14-1/2" wide, 33" high—$2,500.

The "Ridgeway," a 25-year-old walnut reproduction calendar shelf clock, eight-day, time and strike, 15-1/2" wide, 27" high—$300.

Seth Thomas "#10" walnut perpetual-calendar shelf clock with applied and turned decorations. Provisions for the date, day and month are on the lower round tablet, eight-day, time and strike, weight-driven, 36" high—$3,500.

119

Ithaca Calendar Clock Company walnut "Index" (in gold leaf on the glass), with two patent dates, April 18, 1965, and Aug. 28, 1866, perpetual-calendar shelf clock, manufactured for Lynch Brothers with provisions for the date, day and month on the lower round tablet, eight-day, time and strike, 17" wide, 33" high—$2,600.

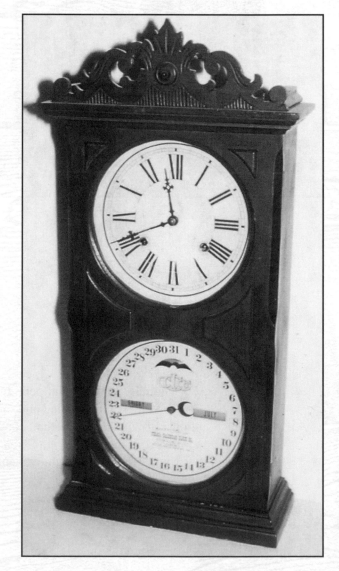

Ithaca Calendar Clock Company "Farmers" walnut perpetual-calendar shelf clock, circa 1865, with Welch movement and provisions for the date, day and month on the lower tablet, eight-day, time and strike, 25-1/2" high—$700.

Ansonia carriage clocks; left, has elliptical dial, 30-hour, time only, 2-1/2" wide, 6" high—$500; right, "Oriole" enameled in colors, with brass frame work, 30-hour, time and alarm, 6-1/2" high—$400.

Carriage clocks, circa 1880 to 1890s: left, Boston Clock Company; middle left, French; middle right, Waterbury repeater; right, Frasier Ipswich, England. All have brass frames and carrying handles, approximately 3-1/2" wide and 4" to 5" high—$350-$450 each.

Boston Clock Company carriage clock, patented Dec. 20, 1880, brass case, porcelain dial, tandem wind-spring movement, 30-hour, time only, 4" wide, 6-1/2" high—$3,000.

Ansonia "Cabinet C" oak shelf clock, brass dial, ormolu decorations, turned oak columns and brass feet, eight-day, time and strike, 11-1/2" wide, 19" high—$800.

Ansonia "The Senator" polished mahogany cabinet clock, antique brass trimmings, silver dial, eight-day, time and half-hour gong strike, 19" wide, 22" high—$2,800.

Ansonia "Cabinet Antique #1" polished mahogany shelf clock, circa 1896, antique brass trimmings, porcelain and brass dial, eight-day, time and half-hour Old English bell strike, 11-1/2" wide, 18-3/4" high—$2,500.

Ansonia "Crystal Palace #1" with two figures under glass dome, mercury pendulum, time and strike, 15" wide, 19" high—$1,500.

Seth Thomas "Prospect #1" mahogany Gothic shelf clock, circa 1910, time and strike, 13-1/2" high—$190.

E.N. Welch rosewood Gothic (beehive) shelf clock, all original, circa 1860 to 1870, 10-1/2" wide, 19" high—$250.

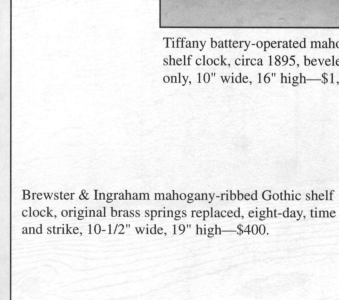

Tiffany battery-operated mahogany Gothic shelf clock, circa 1895, beveled glass, time only, 10" wide, 16" high—$1,200.

Brewster & Ingraham mahogany-ribbed Gothic shelf clock, original brass springs replaced, eight-day, time and strike, 10-1/2" wide, 19" high—$400.

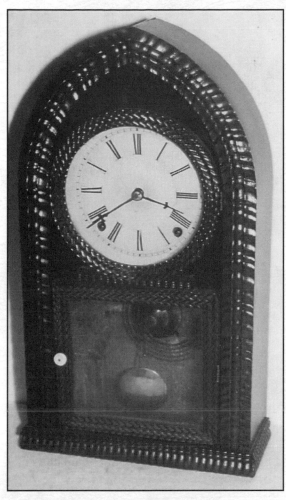

J.C. Brown rosewood ribbed front Gothic shelf clock, circa 1855, time and strike, 10-1/2" wide, 19" high—$900.

J.C. Brown rosewood Gothic shelf clock, circa 1855, dial reads: "J.C. Brown, Forestville Company," replaced tablet, eight-day, time and strike, 10-1/2" wide, 19" high—$300.

Ansonia metal-front dresser clock, porcelain dial, brass case, 30-hour, time only, 3-1/2" wide, 6" high—$165.

Unmarked metal-front mantel clock, porcelain and brass dial, gilted case, 30-hour, time only, 3" wide, 4" high—$135.

Unmarked metal-front mantel clock, patented Oct. 18, 1902, brass case with angel figure at top, 30-hour, time only, 8" wide, 10" high—$70.

French mantel clock, enameled and gilt decorations, circa 1890, eight-day, time only, 12" wide, 15" high—$1,150.

Vincent of Paris mantel clock, circa 1870, with gilt, bronze and white marble and pair of birds on top, eight-day, time and bell strike, 7-1/2" wide, 10" high—$2,885.

German metal-front mantel clock, brass case with eight cast figures, time only, 2-1/2" wide, 6" high—$1,200.

Ansonia metal-front mantel clock, gilted case, porcelain dial, eight-day, time and strike, 7-1/2" wide, 10-1/2" high—$225.

Unmarked metal-front mantel clock, patented Feb. 6, 1904, brass finish, time only, 7-1/2" wide, 11" high—$135.

Seth Thomas metal-front mantel clock, nickel-plated over brass, minute hand, time and alarm, 7" wide, 9" high—$145.

Unmarked metal-front mantel clock with four frogs, one singing, two playing instruments and one sitting at the base of cast-iron case, 30-hour, time only, 9-1/2" wide, 12" high—$250.

Parker Clock Company metal-front mantel clocks, showing cupids carrying clocks, gilted cast-iron cases, 30-hour, time only. Left clock, 6-1/2" high—$300; right clock, 5-1/2" high—$275.

Junghan wooden-grained tambour mantel clock, patented Nov. 9, 1917, German movement, double-hammer strike, eight-day, time and strike, 22" wide, 10-1/2" high—$175.

E. Ingraham miniature (baby camel back) wooden tambour mantel clock, metal dial, 8-1/2" wide, 5-1/2" high—$85.

Seth Thomas wooden case tambour mantel clock, 6-1/2" wide, 3-1/2" high—$85.

W.L. Gilbert oak tambour mantel clock, circa 1880, time and strike, 9-1/2" high—$110.

The Plymouth Clock Company wooden tambour mantel clock, eight-day, time and strike, 19" wide, 9-1/2" high—$125.

Sessions mahogany tambour mantel clock, eight-day, time and strike Westminster chimes, patented 1929, 18" wide, 17-1/2" high—$175.

Seth Thomas adamantine (rosewood finish) tambour mantel clock, eight-day, time and strike, 17-1/2" wide, 10-1/2" high—$245.

Label on back of Seth Thomas tambour mantel clock.

Sessions "Dulciana" mahogany tambour mantel clock, eight-day, time and strike, 21-1/2" wide, 10" high—$175.

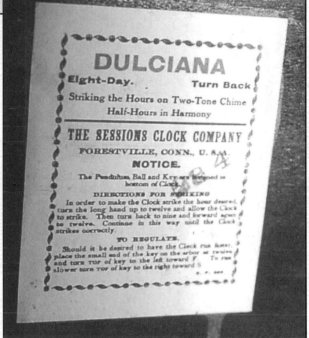

Label on back of Sessions "Dulciana" mantel clock.

Ansonia "Rosalind" cast-iron mantel clock with black-enamel finish, porcelain dial, gilted decorations, seated lady on top, circa 1890, eight-day, time and strike, 15" wide, 19" high—$600.

Ansonia "Minerva" metal mantel clock, circa 1894, with seated lady on top, gilted case, porcelain dial, open escapement, time and strike, 11" wide, 16-1/2" high—$350.

Ansonia "Cygnet" metal mantel clock, circa 1906, with cherub on top holding a wreath, Syrian bronze-finish porcelain dial, eight-day, time and strike, 7-1/2" wide, 12-3/4" high—$395.

Ansonia metal mantel clock with white marbleized case, gilt decorations and copper face, eight-day, time and strike, 11" wide, 18-1/2" high—$500.

Ansonia metal mantel clock with Syrian bronze finish (this finish, as well as Japanese and Berbedienne bronze, produce an aged look) porcelain dial, open escapement, eight-day, time and strike, 11" wide, 17-1/2" high—$550.

Parker Clock Company brass mantel clock with two cupids holding up the lamp post which have jeweled inserts, 30-hour, time only, 7" wide, 6-1/2" high—$800.

E.N. Welch "Albani" marble mantel clock, porcelain dial, open escapement, beveled glass, eight-day, time and strike (contains the famous Patti movement), 14-1/2" wide, 10" high—$550.

Unknown maker, miniature metal mantel clock, corner columns, time only, 4-1/2" wide, 4" high—$115.

E. Ingraham oak mantel clock, circa 1895, time and strike, 10" high—$120.

Ansonia "Capri" cast-iron black-enamel mantel clock, circa 1890, porcelain dial, open escapement, eight-day, time and strike, 15" wide, 12" high—$300.

Ansonia "Denmark" cast-iron black-enameled mantel clock, circa 1890, gold tinted face, three marbleized columns on each side, eight-day, time and strike, 16-1/2" wide, 12" high—$500.

Waterbury mahogany-finished mantel clock, imitation mercury pendulum, glass door with brass frame, eight-day, time and strike, 16-1/2" wide, 9-1/2" high—$225.

French mantel clock, circa 1850 to 1880, with black slate and marble inlay, porcelain dial, open escapement, eight-day, time and strike, 17-1/2" wide, 11-1/2" high—$400.

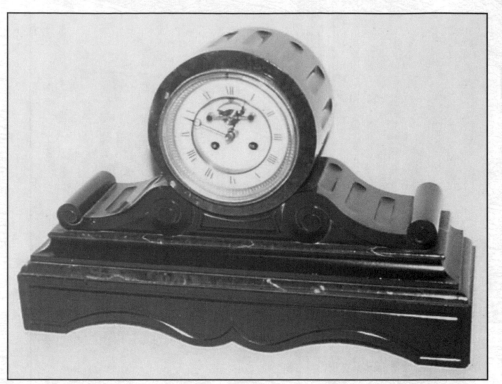

Waterbury cast-iron black-enameled mantel clock, porcelain and brass dial, brass-applied decorations, eight-day, time and strike, 10" wide, 11" high— $300.

Waterbury cast-iron black-enameled mantel clock, brass dial, brass-applied decorations, eight-day, time and strike, 9-1/2" wide, 11" high—$275.

Seth Thomas adamantine (mahogany finish) mantel clock, eight-day, time and strike, 9" wide, 9-1/2" high—$275.

Ansonia "Montague" cast-iron black-enameled mantel clock, circa 1890, porcelain face, gilted decorations, eight-day, time and strike, 13" wide, 12" high—$300.

Ansonia "London Extra" cast-iron black-enameled mantel clock, circa 1895, brass sunburst dial, gilted pillar and lion heads, eight-day, time and strike, 11-1/2" wide, 12-1/2" high—$300.

Seth Thomas adamantine black-enameled mantel clock, circa 1895, with four columns, gilted decorations and marbleized ends, eight-day, time and strike, 18" wide, 12" high—$200.

Ansonia cast-iron black-enameled mantel clock, circa 1890, porcelain dial, open escapement, applied gilted decorations, eight-day, time and strike, 13" wide, 10" high—$275.

Seth Thomas adamantine black-enameled mantel clock, four marbleized columns, copper-wash finish, eight-day, time and strike, 17-1/2" wide, 12" high—$250.

Seth Thomas adamantine brown-finished mantel clock with four marbleized columns, gilted feet and lion heads, eight-day, time and strike, 19" wide, 11-1/2" high—$250.

Seth Thomas adamantine brown-finished mantel clock with four marbleized columns, gilted feet and lion heads, eight-day, time and strike, 16" wide, 12" high— $245.

Seth Thomas adamantine ivory-finished mantel clock with six columns, gilted feet and lion heads, eight-day, time and strike, 17-1/2" wide, 11-1/2" high—$250.

Sessions Clock Co. cherry-stained mantel clock, circa 1910, six columns, gilted feet and lion heads, eight-day, time and strike, 14-1/2" wide, 10-1/2" high—$175.

Seth Thomas adamantine mottled marbleized finish mantel clock, eight-day, time and strike, 17" wide, 12" high—$250.

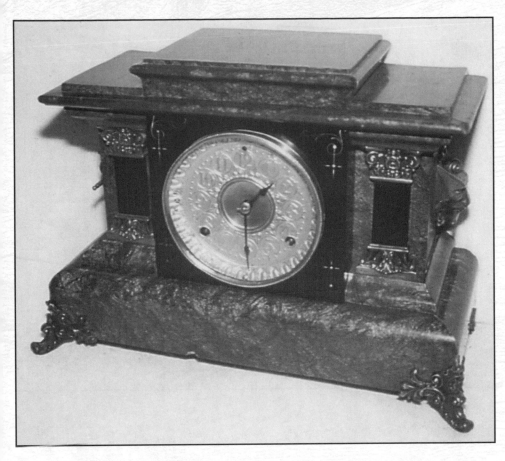

Seth Thomas adamantine mottled gold finish mantel clock, brass dial, 8-hour time and strike, 17" wide, 12" high (paper in back states that this clock was made especially for a company in Rockford, Illinois)—$300.

Ansonia "Carlisle" cast-iron black-enameled mantel clock, circa 1901, gilded pillars, lion heads and feet, eight-day, time and strike, 17" wide, 10" high—$195.

Sessions cast-iron black-enameled mantel clock, gilted pillars, lion heads and feet, 15-1/2" wide, 10-1/2" high—$225.

Sessions cast-iron black-enameled mantel clock, gilted decorations and feet, eight-day, time and strike, 15" wide, 10" high—$175.

Sessions cast-iron black-enameled mantel clock, green pillars, gilted decorations and feet, eight-day, time and strike, 15" wide, 10" high—$165.

Ansonia "Boston Extra" cast-iron black-enameled mantel clock, circa 1890, porcelain dial, open escapement, green pillars, eight-day, time and strike, 15" wide, 11-1/2" high—$300.

Seth Thomas "Arno" adamantine black-enameled mantel clock with gilted and marbleized columns, eight-day, time and strike, 12" wide, 11-1/2" high—$175.

W.L. Gilbert "Curfew" Italian marble finish mantel clock, circa 1910, eight-day, time and bell strike, 16" wide, 17-1/2" high—$375.

Ansonia plush mantel clock, circa 1895, flush dial, beveled glass, gilted winged-dragon feet and lion heads, eight-day, time and strike, 10-1/2" wide, 12-3/4" high—$250.

Ansonia "Unique" black-enameled metal-case mantel clock, circa 1890, slate dial, gilted decorations, eight-day, time and strike, 9-1/2" wide, 10-1/2" high—$250.

Label on back of Ansonia mantel clock. Unusual to have label on this type of clock. It reads, "Prize medal awarded Paris Exposition, 1878…"

Ansonia "Belgium" cast-iron black-enameled mantel clock, circa 1890, porcelain dial, dragons on each end, eight-day, time and strike, 18" wide, 12" high—$400.

French cast-iron mantel clocks: left, elephant, time only, 4" wide, 7" high—$75; right, eagle, time only, 4" wide, 8-1/2" high—$225.

Ansonia "Lisle" cast-iron black-enameled mantel clock, gilt-applied decorations, circa 1890, eight-day, time and strike, 11" wide, 10-1/2" high—$300.

Ansonia "La France" cast-iron black-enameled mantel clock, circa 1890, brass sunburst dial, gilted decorations, eight-day, time and strike, 11-1/2" wide, 11" high—$200.

Ansonia cast-iron black-enameled mantel clock, slate dial, open escapement, four marbleized columns and trim, circa 1890, eight-day, time and strike, 16" wide, 13" high—$500.

Ansonia "Lydia" cast-iron mantel clock, open escapement, with cherubs on top of clock, eight-day, time and strike with matching pair of urns, 19-1/2" high—$2,000.

Ansonia "The Virginia" cast-iron mantel clock with statue, "Opera" on top of clock, open escapement, brass and silver dial, silver panels on each side of clock, eight-day, time and strike, with matching pair of urns, 21" wide, 25" high—$3,500.

Cast-metal ornament for use on flat top clock. Many similar ornaments were available from Ansonia Clock Company, 9" wide, 6" high—$75.

Metal statue decorations of two warriors standing on marble and onyx bases, base 5" x 5", 20" high—no price.

W.L. Gilbert rosewood shelf clock, circa 1860, spring-driven, 13" wide, 19-1/2" high—$250.

Waterbury "Cottage No. 1" mahogany shelf clock, 30-hour, time and strike, 8" wide, 11-3/4" high—$175.

Jerome & Co., mahogany cottage shelf clock, 30-hour, time, strike and alarm, 8" wide, 11-1/2" high—$275.

155

Seth Thomas Plymouth Hollow cottage clock with mother-of-pearl decorated case, eight-day, time and strike, 11" wide, 17" high—$350.

W.L. Gilbert rosewood cottage shelf clock with octagon top, circa 1878-1885, at Winsted, Connecticut, eight-day, time and strike, 10" wide, 13-1/2" high—$165.

E.N. Welch "Empress VP" mahogany shelf clock, simulated mercury pendulum, eight-day, time and strike, 11-1/2" wide, 17-3/4" high—$200.

E.N. Welch "Empress" rosewood shelf clock, circa 1875, eight-day, time and strike, 10-1/2" wide, 16" high—$250.

Left, Ansonia black-case shelf clock, 30-hour, alarm, 7-1/2" wide, 10-1/2" high—$75; right, white shelf clock, 30-hour, time and alarm, 7-1/2" wide, 10-1/2" high—$75.

New Haven "Tuscan" rosewood shelf clock, eight-day, time and strike, 10-1/2" wide, 17-1/2" high—$475.

Jerome & Co., New Haven, Connecticut, walnut shelf clock circa 1855, ebony trim, 30-hour, time and strike, 11-1/2" wide, 16-1/2" high—$225.

Ansonia rosewood Gothic shelf clock, circa 1878, offset pendulum, time only, 10" high—$135.

Ansonia "Harwich" cherry shelf clock, circa 1895, open escapement, ceramic dial, time and strike, 12" high—$225.

Gustav Becker walnut cabinet shelf clock, Westminster chimes, beveled glass, circa 1905, time and strike, 13" high—$325.

English mahogany Gothic shelf clock, with burl inlay, time and strike, circa 1895, 11" high—$265.

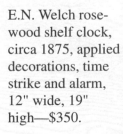

E.N. Welch rosewood shelf clock, circa 1875, applied decorations, time strike and alarm, 12" wide, 19" high—$350.

E. Ingraham walnut and rosewood shelf clock, patented Sept. 30, 1862 (Elias Ingraham's patent date), time and strike, 10-1/2" wide, 14-1/2" high—$395.

Benedict Mfg. Co. mahogany shelf clock, medallion below dial, time only, 3-1/2" wide, 4-3/4" high—$75.

Seth Thomas rosewood cottage shelf clock, circa 1920, time and strike, 13" high—$150.

Jerome & Co. mahogany shelf clock, time and strike with alarm—no price.

Congress walnut cottage shelf clock, circa 1880, eight-hour, time only, 12" high—$150.

Partial label from Jerome & Co. shelf clock.

E. Ingraham oak kitchenette shelf clock, circa 1930, eight-day, time and strike, 13-1/2" wide, 13-1/2" high—$150.

German-made cherry bracket shelf clock, polished brass-embellished dial, beveled glass, circa 1910, time and strike, 15" high—$450.

Close-up of face showing the top dial pendulum adjustment on German-made bracket clock.

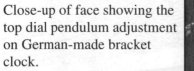

Thwaites & Reed, founded in 1740, Clerkenwell, England rosewood bracket shelf clock with holly inlay, silver dial and brass finials, time only, 15" wide, 21" high—$3,000.

Wurttenburg, Germany, wooden-bracket shelf clock, side lion heads, brass dial, reeded columns and finials, 30-hour, time only, 9" wide, 13" high—$1,650.

Hy Marc, Paris shelf clock, ormolu case, Sevres face, columns and panels; two panels are artist-signed and dated 1897, eight-day, time and strike, 12" wide, 17" high—$3,000.

Ansonia oak shelf clock, brass dial, incised and applied decorations, eight-day, time and strike, 12-1/2" wide, 17" high—$200.

Ansonia "The Herald" enameled wooden case, time and strike, 9-1/2" wide, 16" high—$225.

William S. Johnson, New York, black-enameled papier-mâché case with mother-of-pearl inlay, circa 1895, eight-day, time and strike with winders below the dial, 11" wide, 17" high—$600.

French portico rosewood shelf clock with yew inlay, ormolu decorations and four pillars, time and strike, 12" wide, 22" high—$2,500.

English bracket clock, flame-mahogany case, circa 1860, dial reads, "Archard, London," eight-day, time and strike, double fusee (single fusee does not strike), made by Henry Archard, 13-1/2" wide, 19" high—$2,875.

German mahogany mantel clock, circa 1925, distributed by Russells, Ltd., Liverpool, England, eight-day, time and strike, German movement, 11-1/2" wide, 12-1/2" high—$1,310.

French mahogany shelf clock, early 1900s, with inlaid boxwood, lever platform escapement, eight-day, time only, 10" wide, 20" high—$525.

German oak mantel clock, circa 1910, made by Winterhalder & Hofmeir, silver dial, eight-day, time and strike, 9-1/2" wide, 13-3/4" high—$1,350.

German walnut mantel clock, circa 1900, made by Winterhalder & Hofmeir, eight-day, time and strike, 6-1/2" wide, 10-1/4" high—$2,050.

German-made shelf clocks, circa 1950; first and second on left are brass; the far right clock is plastic; all 30-hour, time only, 4" to 7" height range—$75 each.

German inlaid mahogany mantel clock, circa 1910, German movement by Kienzle, eight-day, time and strike, 7-1/2" wide, 10" high—$535.

French mantel clock with gilt brass and bronze, circa 1850, silver dial, silk suspension, time and strike, 10-1/2" wide, 13-1/2" high—$2,150.

French mantel clock with Belgian slate, often called black marble, bronze spelter horse and figure, made by Le Roy Et Fils of Paris, eight-day, time and strike, 11" wide, 17" high—$1,115.

English black marble or slate mantel clock, circa 1870, with figure of Galileo, eight-day, time and strike, 17-1/2" wide, 13" high—$2,725.

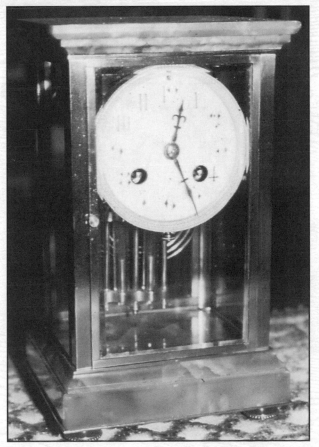

French crystal regulator, circa 1890, onyx base, brass frame, mercury pendulum movement, eight-day, time and strike, 6" wide, 9-1/2" high—$1,475.

French mantel clock, circa 1880, in gray marble, champleve enamel, ormolu decorations and cameo inset, eight-day, time and strike—$3,050.

Lux oak-shelf dresser clock, octagon face, brass dial, 8" wide, 7-1/2" high—$75.

Junghams battery-electric shelf clock, circa 1930-1940, called "1,000 day" clock on the label, 8-1/2" wide, 8-1/2" high—$300.

Back view of Junghams battery electric shelf clock.

German brass battery-electric shelf clocks with glass domes, post World War II, made by Kieninger & Obergfelt, each 9" high—$200 each.

New Haven "Acme" brass shelf clock with top handle, 30-hour, time only—$250.

Waterbury "Hornet" brass shelf clock with ivory dial, glass cylinder, circa 1900, 30-hour, time only, 2-3/4" diameter—$225.

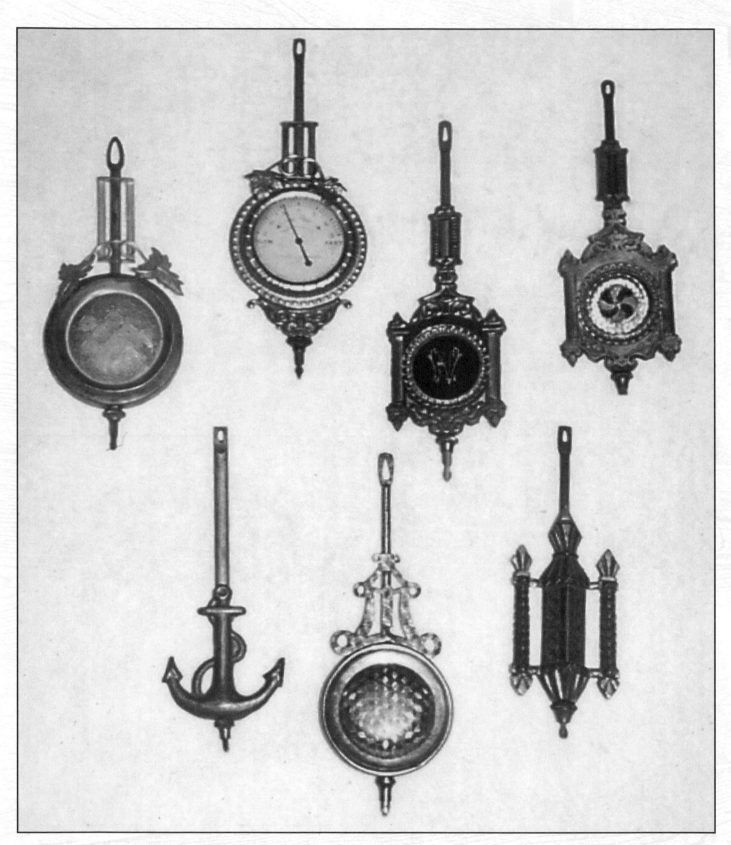

A miscellaneous mixture of pendulums—no price.

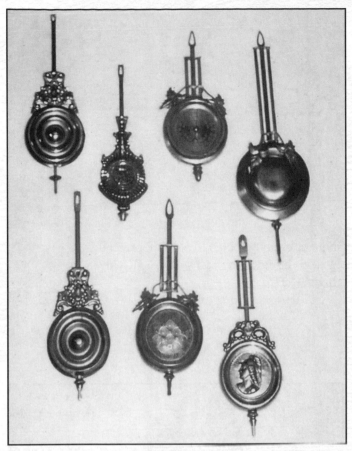

A miscellaneous mixture of pendulums—no price.

Ansonia "Trivoli" oak shelf clock, pressed and applied decorations, brass dial, patented June 18, 1882, eight-day, time and strike, 11-1/2" wide, 15" high—$250.

Ansonia "Dalton" oak shelf clock, circa 1885, incised designs, eight-day, time and strike, 12" wide, 23" high—$255.

Ansonia oak shelf clock, circa 1880, pressed designs, eight-day, time and strike, 15" wide, 23" high—$275.

Ansonia "Triumph" oak shelf clock, circa 1890, mirror sides with brass cupid statues and other applied brass decorations, eight-day, time and strike, 17" wide, 24-1/2" high—$550.

W.L. Gilbert "Pasha" oak shelf clock (part of the Egyptian series), circa 1905, pressed designs, eight-day, time, strike and alarm, 15-1/2" wide, 25" high—$250.

W.L. Gilbert oak shelf clock, circa 1890, incised carving, eight-day, time and strike, 14" wide, 22" high—$200.

W.L. Gilbert oak shelf clock, circa 1901, pressed designs, eight-day, time and strike, 15-1/2" wide, 23" high—$245.

W.L. Gilbert "Mogul" oak shelf clock (part of the Egyptian series), circa 1895, pressed design, eight-day, time, strike and alarm, 16" wide, 24" high—$250.

W.L. Gilbert "Perfect" oak shelf clock, applied decorations and pressed designs, eight-day, time, strike and alarm, 15" wide, 23-1/2" high—$350.

W.L. Gilbert "Egypt" oak shelf clock (part of the Egyptian series), pressed designs, eight-day, time and strike, 17" wide, 25" high—$250.

W.L. Gilbert "Pyramid" oak shelf clock (part of the Egyptian series), pressed designs, eight-day, time and strike, 15-1/2" wide, 24" high—$250.

W.L. Gilbert "Nebo" oak shelf clock, incised designs, eight-day, time, strike and alarm, 11-1/2" wide, 22" high—$250.

E. Ingraham "Post" oak shelf clock, circa 1910, incised designs and applied decorations, eight-day, time and strike, 15" wide, 23" high—$225.

E. Ingraham "Jasper" oak shelf clock, circa 1905, basket weave pressed designs and applied decorations, eight-day, time and strike, 15" wide, 23" high—$250.

E. Ingraham oak shelf clock, pressed designs, eight-day time, strike and alarm, 15" wide, 22" high—$225.

New Haven oak shelf clock with side mirrors, pressed designs, eight-day, time, strike and alarm, 16" wide, 24" high—$350.

Sessions oak shelf clock, circa 1880, pressed designs, eight-day, time and strike, 15" wide, 23" high—$295.

Seth Thomas "Yale" oak shelf clock (part of the College series), incised carving and applied decorations, eight-day, time, strike and alarm, 15" wide, 23" high—$225.

Seth Thomas "New York" oak shelf clock (part of the College series), incised carving and applied decorations, eight-day, time, strike and alarm, 14" wide, 23" high—$250.

Seth Thomas "Cambridge" oak shelf clock (part of the College series; the other three are Cornell, Harvard and Oxford), incised carving and applied decorations, eight-day, time, strike and alarm, 14" wide, 22-1/2" high—$250.

Seth Thomas oak shelf clock (from the metal kitchen series), applied metal decorations, eight-day, time, strike and alarm, 15" wide, 23" high—$250.

Seth Thomas oak shelf clock (from the metal kitchen series), applied metal decorations, eight-day, time, strike and alarm, 15" wide, 22-1/2" high—$250.

Seth Thomas oak shelf clock (from the metal kitchen series), applied metal decorations, eight-day, time, strike and alarm, 14-1/2" wide, 23" high—$250.

Waterbury oak shelf clock, incised carving and applied decorations, simple calendar attachment, eight-day, time and strike, 15" wide, 22" high—$325.

Waterbury "Mansfield" oak shelf clock, circa 1890, incised carving and applied decorations, 15" wide, 21-1/2" high—$225.

Waterbury "Felix" oak shelf clock, circa 1910, incised carving, eight-day, time, strike and alarm, 15" wide, 22" high—$300.

Waterbury oak shelf clock, circa 1899, applied copper decorations, including moose head near top, eight-day, time and strike, 15" wide, 22" high—$265.

Ansonia "Triumph" walnut parlor shelf clock, mirror sides with cupid statues, circa 1890, applied metal decorations, eight-day, time and strike, 17" wide, 24" high—$600.

Ansonia "Mobile" walnut parlor shelf clock, circa 1910, glass sides, circa 1910, incised carving, eight-day, time and strike, 20" high—$495.

W.L. Gilbert "Amphion" walnut parlor shelf clock, three etched beveled mirrors, mirror pendulum, applied decorations, Lincoln drape silk screening on door, 16-1/2" wide, 25" high—$1,500.

Miscellaneous selection of pendulums—no price.

W.L. Gilbert "Attal" walnut parlor shelf clock, incised carvings, eight-day, time, strike and alarm, 20-1/2" high—$285.

W.L. Gilbert "Eastlake" walnut parlor shelf clock, incised carving and applied decorations, eight-day, time and strike, 22" high—$450.

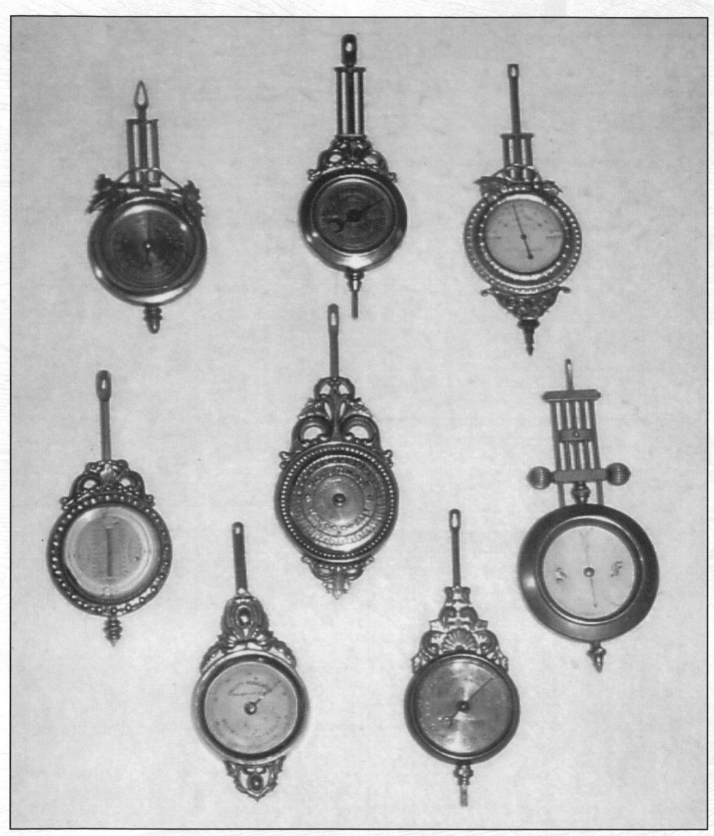

Selection of indicator pendulums, from upper left clockwise: Gilbert, Waterbury, Ansonia, American Clock Company, New Haven, Jarot's, Kroeber and Jarot's in the center with its hand missing—no price.

E. Ingraham walnut parlor shelf clock, incised carving and applied decorations, sharp Gothic-style, eight-day time, strike and alarm, 22" high—$265.

E. Ingraham walnut parlor shelf clock, circa 1890, incised carving, eight-day, time, strike and alarm, 15" wide, 21" high—$225.

E. Ingraham walnut parlor shelf clock, circa 1895, applied decorations, ionic-style, eight-day, time and strike, 22" high—$250.

F. Kroeber "Chalet" walnut parlor shelf clock, circa 1887, pendulum cover removed to expose pendulum, eight-day, time and strike, 17-1/2" high—$265.

F. Kroeber "Mariposa" walnut parlor shelf clock, crystal pendulum bob, eight-day, time and strike, 16" wide, 22-1/2" high—$550.

F. Kroeber "Occidental" walnut parlor shelf clock, circa 1887, mirror sides with brass statues, applied brass decorations, incised carving, turned side columns, cut-glass star bob, eight-day, time and strike, 25" high—$700.

F. Kroeber "Galena" walnut parlor shelf clock, circa 1874, incised carving, applied burl decorations, pewter trim, eight-day, time and strike, 23" high—$440.

F. Kroeber "Kansas" walnut parlor shelf clock, circa 1881, carved drop and upright finials, eight-day, time and strike, 20" high—$425.

F. Kroeber walnut parlor shelf clock, circa 1882, incised carving and applied decorations, eight-day, time and strike, 21" high—$225.

F. Kroeber "Dictator" rosewood parlor shelf clock, circa 1882, 30-hour, time and strike, 17" high—$175.

F. Kroeber "Fearless" walnut parlor shelf clock, circa 1887, incised carving, 30-hour, time and strike, 18" high—$250.

F. Kroeber "Library" walnut parlor shelf clock, burled walnut, applied decorations, indicator pendulum, eight-day, time and strike, 18" wide, 24" high—$1,500.

F. Kroeber "Rambler" walnut parlor shelf clock, circa 1890, incised carving, Jacob's patent "slow and fast" on pendulum, eight-day, time and strike, 11" wide, 20" high—$250.

F. Kroeber "Langtry" walnut parlor shelf clock, incised carving, side pillars and top finials, eight-day, time and strike, 9" wide, 23" high—$800.

Seth Thomas "Tacoma" walnut parlor shelf clock, circa 1870, incised carving, winders under dial, eight-day, time and strike, 23" high—$325.

Seth Thomas walnut-stained parlor shelf clock, side pillars with gilt trim, 8-hour time and strike, 12-1/2" wide, 20" high—$225.

Seth Thomas "Norfolk" walnut parlor shelf clock, circa 1890, incised carving, 8-hour time, strike and alarm, 12" wide, 19-1/2" high—$250.

Seth Thomas "Albany" walnut parlor shelf clock, applied decorations, eight-day, time, strike and alarm, 11" wide, 20-1/2" high—$250.

Seth Thomas walnut parlor shelf clock, circa 1890, incised carving and railing on top, eight-day, time, strike and alarm, 13" wide, 21" high—$250.

Waterbury walnut parlor shelf clock, incised carving, sandwich glass pendulum, 30-hour, time and strike, 12" wide, 18-1/2" high—$150.

Waterbury "Melrose" walnut parlor clock, circa 1881, incised carving, movement is stamped with Waterbury patent, Sept. 22, 1874, eight-day, time and strike, 12-1/2" wide, 21" high—$235.

E.N. Welch "Scalchi" walnut parlor clock (named after Italian operatic soprano), 1884-1893, incised carving, finials, Patti movement, eight-day, time and strike, 12" wide, 19-3/4" high—$1,100.

E.N. Welch "Titiens" walnut parlor shelf clock (named after German soprano, Theresa Titiens), 1877-1884, finials, decorative turnings on stiles, porcelain dial, B.B. Lewis 30-day movement, 30-day time only, 16" wide, 23-1/2" high—$2,200.

Welch, Spring & Co. "The Patti" rosewood parlor shelf clock (named after Spanish operatic prima donna, Adelina Patti), four decoratively turned columns, glass sides, half-hour strike, eight-day, time and strike, 12-1/4" wide, 18-3/4" high—$1,250.

Welch, Spring & Co. "Patti N. 2 VP" or "The Baby Patti" rosewood parlor shelf clock, circa 1889, four decoratively turned pillars, eight-day, time only, double spring, 7-1/2" wide, 10-1/2" high—$3,200.

E.N. Welch "Nanon" walnut parlor shelf clock, circa 1890, incised carving, Sandwich glass pendulum, eight-day, time and strike, 15-1/2" wide, 22" high—$300.

E.N. Welch "Tycon" walnut parlor shelf clock, incised carving, Sandwich glass pendulum, eight-day, time and strike, 14" wide, 23" high—$350.

E.N. Welch "Pepite" walnut parlor shelf clock, circa 1887, incised carving, Sandwich glass pendulum and applied decorations, eight-day, time and strike, 14" wide, 23" high—$300.

E.N. Welch "The Tulip" walnut
parlor shelf clock, incised carving,
13" wide, 19-1/2" high—$175.

E.N. Welch walnut parlor shelf clock, incised
carving, applied decorations, eight-day, time,
strike and alarm, 14" wide, 21" high—$275.

Welch, Spring & Co. walnut parlor shelf clock, incised carving, pendulum reads "E.N.W.," eight-day, time and strike, 12-1/2" wide, 21" high—$275.

E.N. Welch "Roze" walnut parlor shelf clock, incised carving and applied decorations, eight-day, time and strike, 13-1/2" wide, 21" high—$300.

E.N. Welch "Dandelion" walnut parlor shelf clock, incised carving, eight-day, time, strike and alarm, 10" wide, 17-1/2" high—$175.

Collection of nine Welch sandwich glass pendulums. These pendulums have been reproduced and sell for around $20 ($75-$100 each for old ones).

E.N. Welch walnut parlor shelf clock, incised carving, side columns, eight-day, time and strike, 12" wide, 22" high—$275.

Welch, Spring & Co. "Hauck" walnut parlor shelf clock, incised carving, eight-day, time and strike, 14" wide, 22-1/2" high—$350.

E.N. Welch "Litta" walnut parlor shelf clock, incised carving, glass center pendulum, eight-day, time and strike, 16" wide, 23-1/2" high—$350.

E.N. Welch "The Boss" walnut parlor shelf clock, sale tag on back had 1881 date, incised carving, 12-1/2" wide, 20" high—$150.

E.N. Welch "Handel" walnut parlor shelf clock, incised carving, applied decorations, "ENW" embossed on pendulum, eight-day, time and strike, 14" wide, 23" high—$250.

E.N. Welch "Dolaro" walnut parlor shelf clock, circa 1885, incised carving, eight-day, time, strike and alarm, 14" wide, 22-1/2" high—$300.

E.N. Welch "Eclipse" walnut parlor shelf clock, incised carving, eight-day, time, strike and alarm, 15-1/2" wide, 24" high. Originally this clock was a wall hanger, but it was so successful it was changed to a shelf clock. For awhile it was a premium for the Metropolitan Mfg., New York—$350.

E.N. Welch steeple shelf clocks; left, rosewood case, circa 1880, 30-hour, time, strike and alarm, 8" wide, 15" high—$200; right, banded mahogany, circa 1880, 30-hour, time, strike and alarm, 10" wide, 19" high—$200.

Elisha Manross rosewood steeple shelf clock, 30-hour time and strike, 10" wide, 20" high—$170.

J.C. Brown & Company rosewood ripple-front steeple shelf clock, circa 1855, time and strike, 10" wide, 20" high—$1,500.

E.N. Welch mahogany steeple shelf clock, time, strike and alarm, 10" wide, 19-1/2" high—$250.

# Chapter 8
# Novelty Clocks: Timely Tips

In about 1883, a clock produced by the New Haven Clock Company, New Haven, Connecticut, was called "The Craziest Clock in the World," but it was also designated "The best show window attraction ever made." It was called the flying pendulum or "Ignatz" clock. A ball on a string serves as the pendulum. It swings from side to side and winds and unwinds to outer posts. People enjoyed watching it in action.

\* \* \*

The Lux Manufacturing Company began making novelty clocks in Waterbury, Connecticut, as a family project prior to World War I. Current events and comic characters frequently provided the inspiration for amusing clocks. The name deluxe and a distributor, Keebler, are found on some of the clocks. Many Lux clocks were made of compressed molded wood. Plastic and a synthetic marble called "Marblesque" were also used. Lux animated clocks have been extremely popular. Some examples include the Animated Butcher who chops meat while a cat watches; the Organ Grinder and Monkey shows the monkey climbing a fence while the man turns the organ crank; and the Happy Days Animated Clock showing two drinkers over a beer barrel. Lux's pendulette have been produced in large numbers and show unusual objects being substituted for the pendulum. In the Dixie Boy Pendulette, probably one of the most valuable of this type clock, his necktie swings back and forth and the eyes roll from side to side.

\* \* \*

The German clockmakers started the mass-production of clocks in the early part of the 19th century as a result of their sales loses caused by the cheap American clocks that were being shipped to various European countries. Chauncey Jerome was responsible for the many shiploads of these "cheap" clocks that were inundating the German market. The clockmakers copied the American system of mass-production and soon became competitive. They were able to use this approach because one of the younger members of a German family had worked in an American factory.

\* \* \*

When a novelty clock had a dual function, it was called a "two-timer." For example, a cigar cutter and a clock might be combined, or an illuminated alarm clock might be lit by a match when the alarm rang.

\* \* \*

Little attention was given to the oiling and maintenance of clocks until around the middle of the 18th century. As a consequence of this neglect, dirt and dust particles were penetrating the clocks' operating mechanisms. Eventually, clockmakers realized that only if clocks are kept clean would they run accurately. Soon, the mechanisms became totally enclosed.

\* \* \*

A connection with a well known person or a special event may increase a clock's value. For instance, a "Sally Rand" Lux clock also mentions on its pendulum, The Century of Progress 1933 World's Fair in Chicago.

\* \* \*

Three Waterbury novelty clocks, produced in the period between 1874 and 1912, were Sambo, Topsy and Continental. As the pendulum beats, their eyes move up and down. The bodies of these clocks are iron castings by Bradley and Hubbard of Meriden, Connecticut. Other varieties that were available are a dog, lion, organ grinder and Santa Claus. The values of some of these clocks may be in excess of $1,000.

\* \* \*

A unique 30-hour spring-driven novelty clock put out by Nicholas Muller's Sons shows a man pushing a wheelbarrow that contains a clock. It was made in the late 1880s.

\* \* \*

It is amazing to read about the unusual novelty clocks which appeared in the late 1800s and early 1900s. Do you like unusual clocks? How about acquiring a burglar and fire-detective alarm clock? One was produced through the combined efforts of Seth Thomas, Plymouth Hollow and G.K. Proctor & Co. It was patented Aug. 7, 1860. A lamp lights up as soon as the alarm sounds. The clock's rosewood case is 11-1/4" tall.

\* \* \*

An unusual clock brought out by Seth Thomas was a 30-hour ship's bell clock. It has a metal case with a bell beneath. It strikes ship's bells rather than the hours. Other clock manufacturers who made ship's bell clocks were Waterbury and Chelsea Clock Company. The latter was probably the largest producer of this type of clock with the widest variety of styles.

\* \* \*

Examples of novelty clocks are numerous. Of course, there are the 30-hour bobbing doll and its counterpart, the swinging doll timepieces, that Ansonia manufactured in the 1880s. An early 1900s nursery rhyme, "Hickory Dickory Dock" clock had a mouse that ran up the clock. Five models of the mouse clock were made by the New Haven Clock Company. The illustration found in this book was made by Sessions.

* * *

Do you play chess? Do you want to time the intervals between the player's moves? Yale Clock Company's two rectangular tilted clocks, that share a mutual base, check those intervals for you.

Do you need a slot machine clock? Just put your $2.50 gold piece in the slot made for it. This clock with its attractive black wood case, with decorative touches, dates to the early 1900s.

* * *

Would you believe that there was a clock with a translucent milk glass dial that could be hooked on a wall gas clock (the faucet used to turn gas on and off)? This meant that the time could be read at night. When the gas was turned off, this

versatile clock could be placed on a table to provide 24-hour service.

* * *

The Plato by Ansonia told time by turning numbered leaves. It was described as a time indicator by its inventor, Eugene L. Fitch, who patented it in 1902. Two versions of this design can be found in this chapter. The owner of these clocks called them early digital clocks. At one time, replicas were made in Germany.

Keebler cuckoo pendulette, molded wood, green-colored leaves, 30-hour, time only, spring-driven, 3-1/2" wide, 6" high—$55.

Keebler cuckoo pendulette, molded wood, red and green foliage, 30-hour, time only, spring-driven, 5" wide, 6-1/2" high—$45.

Lux cuckoo pendulette, molded wood, bird sitting on the top, 30-hour, time only, spring-driven, 4" wide, 6" high—$45.

Lux cuckoo pendulette, molded wood, bird sitting at the top, 30-hour, time only, spring-driven, 8-1/2" wide, 11-1/2" high—$200.

Lux cuckoo pendulette, molded wood, bird sitting at the top, 30-hour, time only, spring-driven, 4-1/2" wide, 7" high—$55.

Keebler pendulette, molded wood, spread-winged eagle at the top, green leaves, 30-hour, time only, spring-driven, 4" wide, 5" high—$45.

Keebler cuckoo pendulette, molded wood, 30-hour, time only, spring-driven, 4" wide, 5" high—$45.

Lux cuckoo pendulette, molded wood, green leaves and bluebird, time only, spring-driven, 4" wide, 5" high—$45.

Keebler cuckoo pendulette, molded wood, green leaves and red flowers, bluebird feeds its babies, 30-hour, time only, spring-driven, 4" wide, 5" high—$45.

Lux cuckoo pendulette with original box marked, "Lux Pendulette Clock-a Novelty Clock by Lux," 30-hour, time only, spring-driven, 4" wide, 7" high—$125.

Keebler "Coo-Coo" clock in original box, never used, molded wood, 30-hour, time only, 4-1/2" wide, 7" high—$125.

Lux wooden clock featuring girl and soldier on blue base, 30-hour, time only, spring-driven, 9" wide, 7" high—$800.

The top of a shipping crate used for shipping Lux clocks, 26" wide, 15-1/2" high—no price.

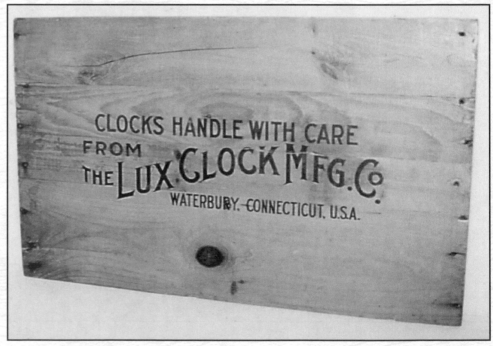

Lux Good Luck metal clock featuring a "Horse Shoe" surrounding the clock, 30-hour, time only, 9" wide, 7-1/2" high—$50.

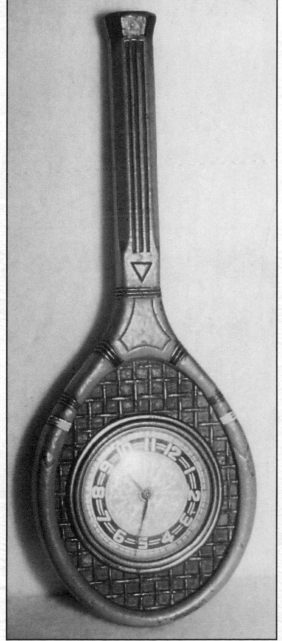

Lux "Tennis Racket" clock, 30-hour, time only, 3" wide, 7-1/2" high—$100.

Lux "Show Boat" clock with paddle wheel that turns, 30-hour, time only, 5" wide, 4-1/2" high—$125.

Lux "Happy Days" clock, showing two drinkers standing next to a "3 Point 2" beer barrel, 30-hour, time only, 4" wide, 4" high—$125.

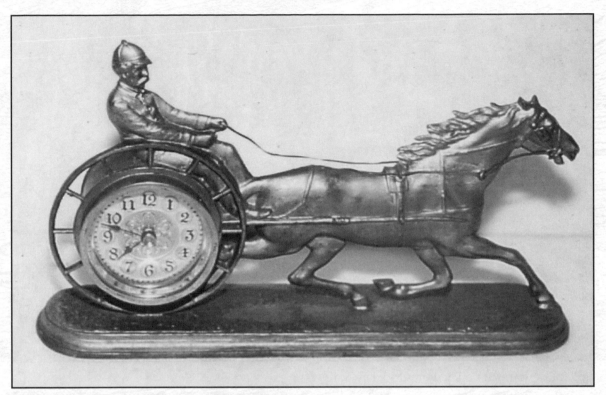

Ansonia brass trotter novelty clock, 30-hour, time only, 10-1/2" wide, 6-1/2" high—$600.

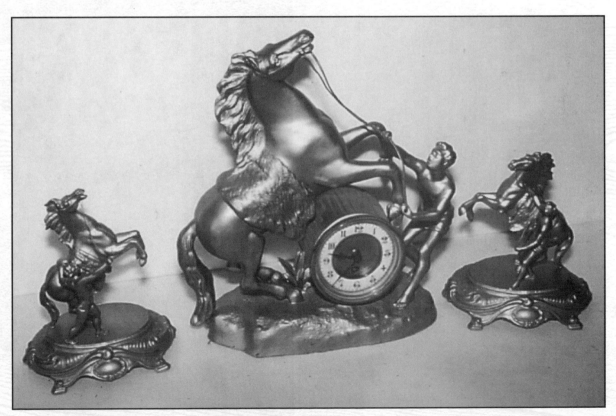

Maker unknown, three-piece set of horses with the center one holding the clock, circa 1890, gold finish, porcelain dial, beveled glass, eight-day, time only, 12" wide, 15-1/2" high—$650.

Two animal clocks; left, Russell & Jones "Jockey," silver-plated, 30-hour, time only, 7-3/4" wide, 7" high—$400; right, Jennings Brothers Mfg. Co. bull dog, novelty clock, gilt finish, patented Jan. 13, 1891, Bridgeport, Connecticut, 30-hour, time only, 8" wide, 6" high—$300.

F. Kroeber owl novelty clock, glass eyes, 30-hour time and alarm, 6" wide, 10" high—$400.

German wooden novelty clocks of three dogs with eyes that mark the time, 30-hour, time only, 5" to 6" high—$200-$300 each.

New Haven ball watch hanging on eagle stand with onyx base, 30-hour, time only, 9" high— $850.

Ansonia novelty clocks; left, "Novelty #23 Peacock" with embossed metal surround and appendages, 30-hour, time only 2" dial, 7-1/2" high—$450; right, "Novelty #20 Birds," metal, 30-hour, time only, 2" dial, 4-1/2" high—$375.

Ansonia novelty clocks; left, squirrel in a tree, enameled pot metal, 30-hour, time only, 7" wide, 6" high—$400; right, clock in a brass frame featuring two robins, one of which is feeding the babies in a nest, 30-hour, time only, 5-1/2" wide, 7" high—$200.

Ansonia metal novelty clocks; left, "Novelty 34," also called "The Advertiser," because there is space for ads above and below the dial, 30-hour, time only, 7" high—$500; right, "Novelty 15" with owl supporting clock, 30-hour, time only, 2" dial, 6" high—$500.

Ansonia metal novelty clocks; left is "Train Novelty #44," patented April 23, 1878, 30-hour, time only, 2" dial, 7-3/4" high—$600. Right is "Cat Novelty #52," 30-hour, time only, 2" dial, 9" high—$850.

German wooden novelty owl clock, sitting on a book, where moving eyes tell time, circa 1920s. The left eyeball line indicates the hour and the right eye shows the minutes rotating to the right, 4" wide, 6-1/2" high—$600.

Sessions wooden Dickory, Dickory Dock clock has a white mouse running up and down the time line, eight-day, time only, 35" high—$500.

E.N. Welch "Rosebud" clock with an angel and flowers inscribed on the brass clock surround, 30-hour, time only, 6" wide, 7" high—$200.

Ansonia metal novelty clocks; left, Black Man beating time, 30-hour, time only, 2" dial, 5" high—$1,000; right, "Novelty #48" of children sledding, 30-hour, time only, 6" wide, 6-3/4" high—$800.

Ansonia brass novelty clocks; left, "Swing #1" doll, 30-hour, time only, 4" dial, 11-1/2" high—$2,000; right, "Swing #2" doll, 30-hour, time only, 4" dial, 8" high—$1,800.

Ansonia metal novelty doll clocks; left, "Jumper #1," 30-hour, time only, 4" dial, 15-1/2" high—$1,800; right, "Jumper #2," 30-hour, time only, 4" dial, 14-1/2" high—$1,600.

Ansonia cast-iron black-enamel novelty mantel clock, with a ship's brass wheel rotating as the escapement moves, seen in 1894 catalogue, 15" wide, 18-3/4" high—$2,000.

Ansonia metal bouncing doll, patent date on dial is Dec. 14, 1886, original German doll, 15-1/2" high—$1,300.

Mastercrafters plastic-case
novelty clock with boy and
girl swinging as time ticks,
time only—$175.

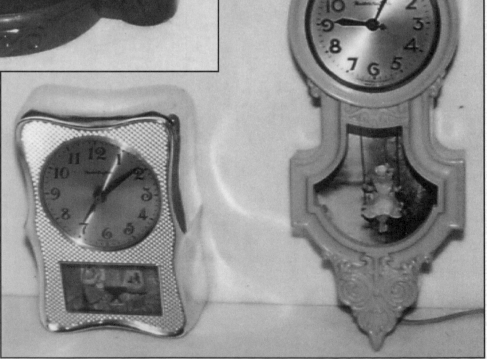

Mastercrafters electric
novelty clocks; left, animated
blacksmith—$85; right, girl
swinging—$145.

F. Kroeber bronzed novelty clock with Kroeber movement; girl swings to and fro by utilizing Kroeber's double escapement wheel on the pendulum rod; Egyptian lady's head above dial, eight-day, time only, 5" wide, 19" high—$1,500.

Waterbury wooden and metal novelty clock showing boy with saw, patented Jan. 13, 1891, 30-hour, time only, 8-1/2" wide, 10-1/2" high—$600.

British brass novelty clock showing a bicycle and delivery man, often called a "Western Union clock," registered 1893, Birmingham, 30-hour, time only, 8" wide, 6-1/2" high—$1,000.

F. Kroeber pot metal and walnut Angel Swing novelty parlor clock, circa 1876, reconditioned case, eight-day, time only, 19-1/2" high—$2,600.

Ansonia metal novelty clocks with porcelain dials, eight-day, time only. Small figure—$650; large figure—$600.

Ansonia brass novelty clocks; left, Cupid riding a snail, 30-hour, time only, 5" high—$275; right, baby holding a fan, 30-hour, time only, 5" high—$375.

F. Kroeber "Sheffield" walnut miniature novelty shelf clock, circa 1890, time only, 20" high—$190.

Left, Lux rotary metal tape measure novelty clock, circa 1910, copper finish, time only, 5" diameter—$45; right, Westclox Big Ben alarm clock, patented 1914—$65.

Pallwebber's digital pendulum patent used in this walnut novelty shelf clock. There is a second-hand and two windows that display the hours and minutes, beveled glass, eight-day, time only, 12" wide, 13" high—$750.

Waterbury walnut-stained novelty shelf clock with a hand that goes up and down and rotates at the top and bottom to show time on this elongated dial, eight-day, time only, 13-1/2" wide, 15" high—$500-$600.

Timby Solar walnut novelty shelf clock with a world globe that rotates to indicate the hours; base dial rotates to register the minutes, time only, only 600 made, 14" wide, 27" high— $4,000-$5,000.

German lighthouse novelty shelf clock that tells the time on the lower square brass dial; the eight single hand-time discs tell time in Greenwich, New York, San Francisco, Paris, Peking, Madrid, Amsterdam and Petersburg. The door in back opens up to wind the clock, 21-1/2" high. Runs on a ladder chain. (The first American lighthouse clock, 1822, was attributed to Simon Willard)—$2,000.

Unknown maker, brass Masonic emblem novelty desk clock, circa 1910, time only, 6-1/2" high—$190.

Ansonia metal novelty shelf clocks; left is "Twins," 30-hour, time only, movement patented March 27, 1877, 3" dial, 10-1/2" high—$400. Right is "The Jug," 30-hour, time only, 3" dial, 10" high—$200.

Ansonia "The Sonnet" brass-framed novelty shelf clock, with knight's head on velvet background, eight-day, time only, tandem spring drive, 20-1/2" high—$1,500.

Minneapolis-Honeywell Regulator Co. combination metal clock and thermometer, eight-day, time only, seven-jewel model, 2-1/2" dial, 10" high—$55.

Brewster & Ingraham walnut open case showing its brass east-west movement, 15" diameter—$300.

German walnut-stained novelty shelf clock, door pulls down to open, ceramic face, time only, spring-driven, 8" wide, 12-1/2" high—$160.

New Haven brass dresser clock, porcelain dial, 3" diameter, time only—$85.

German enameled novelty wall clock, circa 1920s, green and white finish, eight-day, time only, 6" wide, 7" high—$135.

Herschede-movement American
novelty shelf clock, seven jewels,
circa 1900, eight-day, time only, 7"
diameter—$250.

Unknown maker, multi-colored wooden pendulette,
cuckoo clock, 30-hour, time only, spring-driven—$45.

E.N. Welch metal suitcase novelty clock, copper-finished, 30-hour, time only, 3" wide, 3" high—$150.

Ansonia "Eva" novelty shelf clock with brass surround, patented 1892, porcelain dial, beveled mirror, eight-day, time only, 8" wide, 9-1/2" high—$600.

Thames Mercer Chronometer, in wooden case, St. Albans, England, circa 1830, made for ship's clocks, three-day marine chronometer on a gimble fusee, 7-1/4" wide, 7-1/2" high—$2,200.

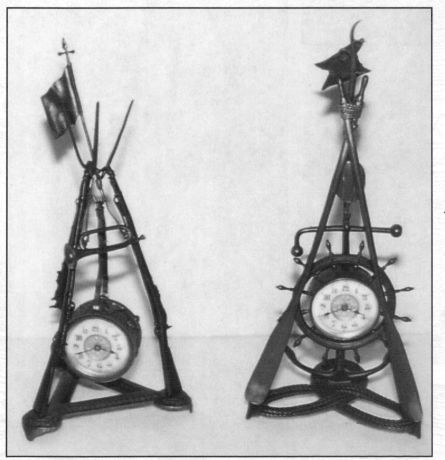

Ansonia metal novelty clocks with jeweled settings; left, "Army," with rifle supports, antique brass, gilt center, porcelain dial, one-day, time only, 2" dial, 12" high—$450; right, "Navy," with oar supports, antique brass, gilt center, porcelain dial, one-day, time only, 2" dial, 12" high—$450.

245

Unknown maker, metal Ferris Wheel novelty clock, souvenir of the Paris 1900 Exposition (printed on tablet); as the clock runs, the Ferris Wheel turns, time only, 5" wide, 11-1/2" high—$800.

A second example of the Ferris Wheel novelty clock with a plain tablet—no price.

Kline & Company, New York, "#602" chronometer in a wooden case, circa 1830, fusee-operated, 7-1/4" wide, 7-1/2" high—$2,200.

Left, E.N. Welch metal suitcase novelty clock, copper washed, 30-hour, time only, 3" wide, 2" high—$400; right, Waterbury brass-finished novelty clock on stand with two Black figures standing by bale of cotton which serves as a match holder, 30-hour, time only, 6" wide, 5" high—$600.

New Haven fan novelty clock with brass stand and decorations, porcelain and brass dial, 30-hour, time only, 13" wide, 8" high—$600.

Abra Clock Co., Geneva, Switzerland, battery novelty clock, time only, 3" wide, 4" high—$275.

Left, Ansonia metal anchor and ship's wheel novelty clock, time only, 9" high—$500; right, Ansonia metal novelty clock with a sailor sitting on a rope under the clock which is supported by a pair of oars, time and alarm, 8" high—$500.

Hawkeye Clock Company's "Muscatine Timer," 30-hour, time only, 4" wide, 6" high—$75.

Year Clock Company, New York, mahogany-case novelty clock that runs a year, patented 1903, 4" dial—$600.

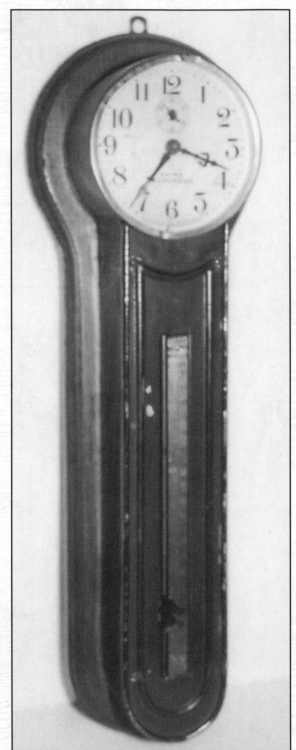

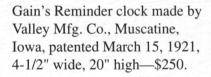

Gain's Reminder clock made by Valley Mfg. Co., Muscatine, Iowa, patented March 15, 1921, 4-1/2" wide, 20" high—$250.

Unknown maker, electrically operated, plastic windmill shelf novelty clock with moving blades, circa 1940, time only, 8-1/2" high—$100.

Unknown maker (probably foreign), mahogany-finished four-column novelty shelf clock, porcelain dial, time only, 6-1/2" diameter dial, 13" high—$250.

W.L. Gilbert wooden religious mass clock, 5" wide, 6" high—$125.

Unknown maker, of reproduction Flying Pendulum novelty clock; original patent date was 1883, 7" wide, 10" high—$100.

Sentinola kitchen-call clock tells when something is done, like a timer, 7-1/2" wide, 7" high—$50.

United Metal Goods Mfg. Co. Inc. electric carriage novelty clock, patent 1938, 13" wide, 9" high— $95.

Left, E.N. Welch nickel-plated novelty shelf clock, time only, 3" wide, 2" high—$200; right, E.N. Welch novelty clock, shaped like a watch, souvenir from 1893 Chicago World's Fair, 30-hour, time only, 3" diameter. Inscription on back reads: "Landing of Columbus in America October 12th 1492"—$300.

E.N. Welch jewel novelty clocks; left, amber, patented 1881, 30-hour, time only, 4" wide, 4" high—$200; right, crystal, 30-hour, time only, 4" wide, 4" high—$200.

Ansonia metal novelty clocks; left, "Simmons Liver Regulator" on horseshoe surround, 30-hour, time only, 6" high—$400; right, "Pearl," 30-hour, time only, 4" diameter dial, 6-1/2" high—$200.

Mastercrafters collection of electric novelty clocks, popular in the 1940s; top row, from left—$125 (girl); $175 (boy and girl); $125 (girl); $100 (bird); bottom row, from left—$90 (church); $55 (waterfalls); $90 (church chimes); $65 (fireplace).

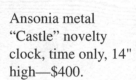

Ansonia metal "Castle" novelty clock, time only, 14" high—$400.

Ansonia metal "Ship" novelty clocks with cupid figure on each, 30-hour, time only. The middle ship is 13" high and other two are 9" high—$350 each.

Left, Ansonia Plato Design #2 early digital novelty clock, patented 1903, time only, 6-1/2" high; right, Design #4 early digital novelty clock, patented 1903, time only, 6-1/2" high—no price.

Ansonia brass jeweled novelty clocks: left, "The Harp" 30-hour, time only, 1-1/2" dial, 9" high—$500; right, "The Token," porcelain dial, gilt center, two cupids within heart design, 30-hour, time only, 1-1/2" dial, 5-1/2" high—$400.

J.E. Buerk, Boston, made the first time clock, patented 1861, brass with leather case, 3-1/4" diameter—$700.

Lux novelty shelf clock, showing fire-place scene with turning spinning wheel, 30-hour, time and alarm, 4-1/2" wide, 5" high—$125.

Wood, gesso and plaster Swedish novelty wall clock, circa 1880, in green, gold and red colors, eight-day, time and strike, 15" wide, 25" high—$350.

Ansonia "Bee" clock shown with its original shipping tin, circa 1890, time only, 2" dial—$100.

Ansonia Means "Square Pirate" clock with original cardboard box, 4" wide, 4" high—$60.

# Chapter 9
# *Wall Clocks: Timely Tips*

During the Victorian Era (named for England's Queen Victoria who reigned from 1837 to 1901), ornate carvings on household furnishings, including clocks, were in vogue. Both drop and upright carved finials, curved moldings and carvings including heads, abounded in the latter half of the 1800s. Incised carvings prevailed around 1870. While oak and mahogany were used at times, walnut was the dominant wood selected by clockmakers in the latter half of the 1800s.

\* \* \*

The pendulum is a clock weight, often ornamental, hung from a fixed point so it can swing to and fro as it regulates the clock's movement. Brooks Palmer in his book, *The Book of American Clocks*, reminds readers that the term "bob" is commonly used but incorrectly defined. He points out that a pendulum "has three parts—the pendulum rod and the pendulum ball which most people call the bob and the real bob which is the wire loop threaded for the regulating nut." The ball (or as commonly called the bob) is often ornamental as well as necessary. It is the weight at the end of the pendulum rod. It may be round or geometrical in shape. It can be engraved or have leaf appendages. A man's head in low relief or a woman's portrait might adorn a pendulum. Crystal, sandwich glass (made in layers) and wooden examples are found. The French made genuine mercury pendulum bobs, while American examples were an imitation mercury. As the time-line indicates, Christaan Huygens was first to create a practical pendulum, circa 1657. Italy's Galileo (1504-1642)

thought a pendulum was possible based on his observations of a swinging lamp.

\* \* \*

Octagon clocks hung on walls in schools, offices and churches. They are often referred to as school house clocks. They were also popular in warehouses.

\* \* \*

Years ago, railroad depots traditionally used regulator clocks with their precise mechanism to make sure trains ran on a schedule. These clocks also frequently appeared in jewelry windows as a advertising lure. Clock and watch repairers and passers by could determine whether their timepieces were functioning correctly by checking them with the regulator's time.

\* \* \*

Gallery clocks, made since 1845, were designed for use in public places. They have large, round dials that can be seen readily. Currently made examples are either eight-day or electric.

\* \* \*

From 1890 to 1896, Edward P. Baird of Plattsburgh, New York, made papier-mâché advertising clocks containing Seth Thomas movements. From around 1896 to 1900, he made wooden clocks with embossed or painted advertisements around the metal dial.

\* \* \*

Around 1885, in New York, the Sidney Advertiser Company, was in operation. It manufactured a clock that had a bell that rang and advertising drums that turned every five minutes. Complete clocks are hard to find. However, missing drums can be replaced by reproduction ones.

Hanging shelf clocks appear to be sitting on shelves when, in reality, they are actually hanging on the wall.

\* \* \*

Gustav Stickley's Mission-style furniture had stoic, straight, sturdy lines. Oak was his favorite wood. He also made accessory articles, including clocks. The Mission-style was in vogue from the turn of the century until the 1920s. Interest in this style revived in the 1960s when both authentic Mission furniture and reproductions became available.

\* \* \*

In England, around 1660, a calendar movement was put in a tall-case clock to create a calendar clock. In 1853, J.H. Hawes, of Ithaca, New York, was the first known American to patent a simple calendar clock mechanism. In 1865, the Ithaca Calendar Clock Company was formed. It used Henry B. Horton's perpetual roller-type calendar clock patent.

\* \* \*

A perpetual calendar clock indicates the day of the week, the month and the date. It is self-adjusting to allow for leap year. A simple calendar clock, however, requires an occasional manual adjustment to make it accurate.

\* \* \*

The 1881 Waterbury Perpetual Calendar Clocks could be furnished with months and days of the week in English, Spanish, Portuguese, French, German, Swedish and Italian.

\* \* \*

Charles W. Feishtinger developed a calendar dial that showed the day of the week, month of the year and date of the month. The dates circled the dial by the outer rim and were marked by a sweep hand. The months were marked by a short hand in the middle of the main dial. The days were indicated by a rectangular window beneath he month dial. He used Waterbury's movement and case to enclose his calendar mechanism.

\* \* \*

The Ithaca Fashion calendar dial shows the dates of the month by numbers encircling the outer rim of the dial, while the day of the week and the month of the year are shown in two rectangular windows in the middle left and right of the main dial.

\* \* \*

Jerome & Co. clock labels were used on many New Haven clocks and do not relate to the earlier Chauncey Jerome Company.

\* \* \*

The word regulator was originally used to designate an accurate wall clock, one that was often used in jewelry stores where precise times were necessary. These regulators demonstrated superior mechanism and were made to give split-second accuracy. They were used also for the regulation of other time-keepers. A great number of clocks called regulators or named "regulator" on their tablets are not accurate enough to be so classified. In these cases, it has become a generic, look-a-like term for a hanging clock.

\* \* \*

Waterbury produced a series of oak hanging study clocks, weight- or spring-driven, commonly called "Wag-on-Wall" clocks. Waterbury used the word "Study" and numbers from 5 through 11 to classify these Wag-on-Walls. Gideon Roberts (1749-1813) made an all wooden one in the late 1700s. They resemble a clock without a case and are the earliest wall clocks made. Metal plates enclose the movement, but the pendulum is exposed and swings back and forth beneath the body of the clock.

\* \* \*

Connecticut wall clocks were made in large numbers for use in schools, offices, churches and public buildings. Examples of these include octagons, galleries and figure-eight or ionic clocks.

In an early 1900s Ansonia catalog, it featured hanging clocks named after female regents including the following: Queen Charlotte, Queen Elizabeth, Queen Jene, Queen Mary, Queen Isabelle and Queen Anne. The were available in eight-day, strike, had 8" dials and averaged between 37" to 42" in height. Woods available were black walnut, a dark wood, mahogany or oak. Any of the clocks could be purchased for well under $20.

E. Ingraham wall clock advertising Ever-Ready Safety Razor, time only, 18" diameter, 29" high—$3,500.

Ithaca Calendar Clock Company "#1" walnut perpetual-calendar wall clock with H.B. Horton's patents, April 18, 1865, and Aug. 28, 1866, and provisions for the date, day and month on the lower tablet, sweep secondhand, double weight-driven, time only, 19" wide, 6 feet high— $15,000.

Bulova electric wall clock, 16" wide, 16" high—$110.

Coca-Cola electric wall clock, 16" wide, 16" high—$110.

Sessions walnut Jeweler's regulator wall clock, 1902, advertising Weiler's Music Store, Quincy, Illinois, circa 1902, time only, 38-1/2" high—$650.

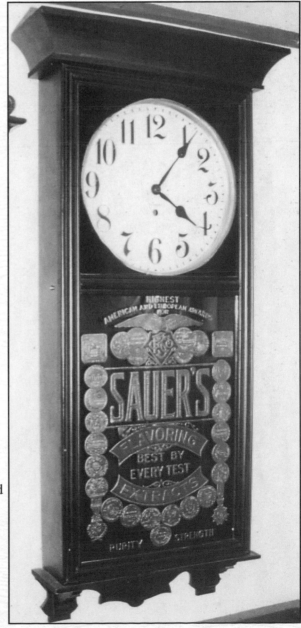

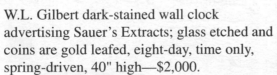

W.L. Gilbert dark-stained wall clock advertising Sauer's Extracts; glass etched and coins are gold leafed, eight-day, time only, spring-driven, 40" high—$2,000.

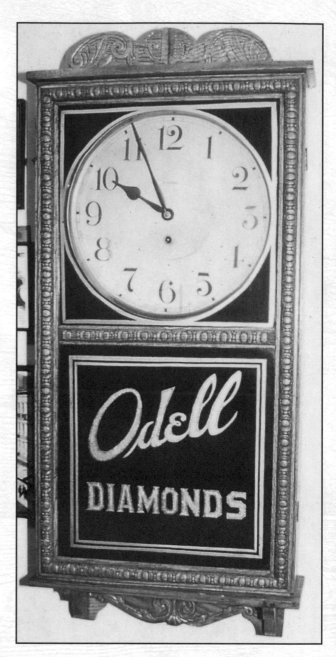

Waterbury oak Jeweler's regulator wall clock advertising Odell Jewelry Store, Quincy, Illinois, time only, 37" high—$650.

Sessions walnut-stained wall clock, circa 1903, advertising La Reforma Havana Cigars, repainted tablet, eight-day, time only, spring-driven, 16-1/2" wide, 38" high—$500.

Ithaca Calendar Clock Company "Belgrade" walnut perpetual-calendar wall clock, patented 1866, wooden bob and provisions for the date, day and month on the lower tablet, W.H. Kelley Jewelry on dial, eight-day, time and strike, 14" wide, 38" high—$2,800.

Ithaca Calendar Clock Company "Kildare" mahogany perpetual-calendar wall clock, intricate case carving, sweep secondhand and provisions for the date, day and month on the lower tablet, cut crystal bob, eight-day, time and strike, 13" wide, 33" high—$4,800.

Welch, Spring & Co. "#2" rosewood perpetual-calendar wall clock with provisions on the upper dial for the days of the week marked by a small hand and on the lower dial for the days indicated by a large hand and the months marked with a small hand. It has the Lewis patented calendar mechanism and is eight-day, time only, 13" wide, 34" high—$1,400.

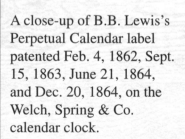

A close-up of B.B. Lewis's Perpetual Calendar label patented Feb. 4, 1862, Sept. 15, 1863, June 21, 1864, and Dec. 20, 1864, on the Welch, Spring & Co. calendar clock.

Seth Thomas "#5" walnut perpetual-calendar wall clock with secondhand, applied walnut decorations; calendar details found on lower dial, time only, weight-driven, 50" high—$6,000.

E. Ingraham Company walnut-stained simple calendar wall clock with calendar dates on upper dial, eight-day, time only, 12" wide, 24" high—$525.

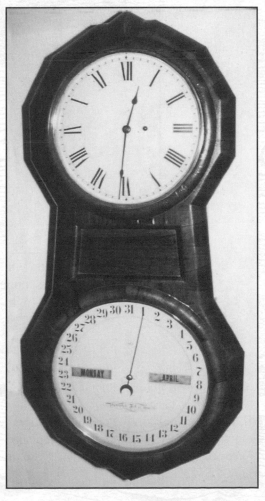

Seth Thomas "#1" rosewood perpetual-calendar wall clock, patented 1876, eight-day, time only, weight-driven, 40" high—$3,000.

Ithaca Calendar Clock Company cast-iron ionic perpetual-calendar wall clock using H.B. Horton's calendar movement as seen on bottom dial, eight-day, time only, 9" wide, 19" high—$2,500.

New Haven embossed oak simple calendar
wall clock, circa 1910, eight-day, time only,
17" wide, 28" high—$450.

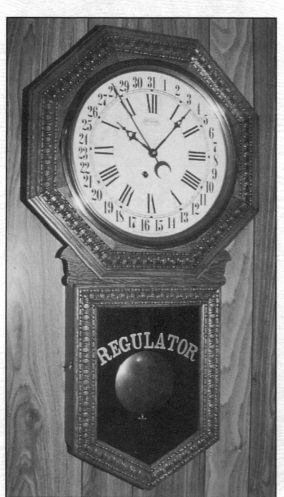

W.L. Gilbert "Office" walnut simple calendar
octagon wall clock, applied decorations, eight-day,
time and strike, 32" high—$900.

E. Ingraham oak simple calendar octagon wall
clock, circa 1910; face and tablet replaced with
exact copy, eight-day, time only, 18" wide, 32"
high—$425.

Seth Thomas "Office #11" mahogany perpetual-calendar wall clock, patented 1876, eight-day, time only, weight-driven, 68-1/2" high—$12,500.

Sessions walnut simple calendar wall clock, circa 1890, eight-day, time only, 39" high—$550.

E.N. Welch oak simple calendar wall clock, circa 1890, eight-day, time only, 18" wide, 40" high—$600.

German cuckoo wall clock, West Germany chalet-style, circa 1950, 30-hour, 9" wide—$225.

Unknown maker,
oak mission wall
clock, exposed
pendulum, 13" wide,
26" high—$295.

German cuckoo wall clock, circa 1920, 30-
hour, 13" wide, 30" high—$300.

Waterbury oak regulator wall clock, circa
1912, secondhand, time only, weight-
driven, 37" high—$1,100.

Seth Thomas "#60" mahogany regulator wall clock, brass pendulum and weight, eight-day, time only, weight-driven, 18-1/4" wide, 60" high—$10,750.

New Haven "Office #1" walnut regulator wall clock, circa 1886, secondhand, time only, single weight-driven, 42" high—$1,000.

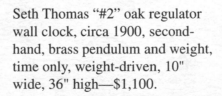

Seth Thomas "#2" oak regulator wall clock, circa 1900, second-hand, brass pendulum and weight, time only, weight-driven, 10" wide, 36" high—$1,100.

Seth Thomas "#60" mahogany wall clock, sweep secondhand, brass weight, eight-day, time only, 14" dial, 58-1/2" high—$10,000.

Seth Thomas "#18" walnut wall clock, nickel-plated pendulum and weight, eight-day, time only, weight-driven, 14" dial, 54" high—$2,700.

Seth Thomas "#1" rosewood regulator wall clock, circa 1855, round top, secondhand, eight-day, time only, weight-driven, 11" dial, 34" high—$2,000.

Seth Thomas "#1 Extra" walnut regulator, circa 1875, secondhand, time only, weight-driven, 13-1/3" dial, 40" high—$2,000.

Seth Thomas "#3" walnut wall clock, secondhand, "Ball Watch Co., Cleveland" on dial, time only, weight-driven, 14" dial, 44" high—$3,000.

Seikosha Japanese dark-stained regulator wall clock, circa early 1900s, eight-day, time and strike, 14" dial, 51" high—$350.

Unknown maker, miniature school house type, dark-stained wall clock, patented 1920, time only, spring-driven, 5" dial, 14-1/2" high—$250.

Japanese artificially grained ionic wall clock, with ebony and gilt trim, circa 1900, time and strike, spring-driven, 8" dial, 19" high—$250.

E.N. Welch "Alexis #1" rosewood ionic wall clock, circa 1880, applied gold leaf on tablet, eight-day, time only 12" dial, 26" high—$400.

Waterbury "Para" rosewood ionic wall clock, circa 1891, time only, 10" dial, 22" high—$375.

E.N. Welch "Alexis #2" ebony-decorated rosewood wall clock, circa 1875, applied gold leaf on tablet, eight-day, time only, 10" dial, 22" high—$350.

Waterbury "Baha" gilted ionic wall clock, circa 1900, time and strike, 13" wide, 21" high—$350.

E.D. Vimpany, Dover, mahogany wall clock, circa 1860, single fusee, time only, 12" dial—$1,150.

Ansonia walnut short drop-stained wall clock, 30-day, time only, 11" dial, 24" high—$350.

Waterbury "Union" walnut wall clock, pictured in its 1892 catalogue, eight-day, spring-driven—$495.

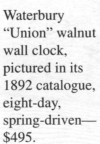

Elliott & Co. English rosewood trunk, dial wall clock, single fusee movement, circa 1941, RAF insignia on dial, 14" dial—no price.

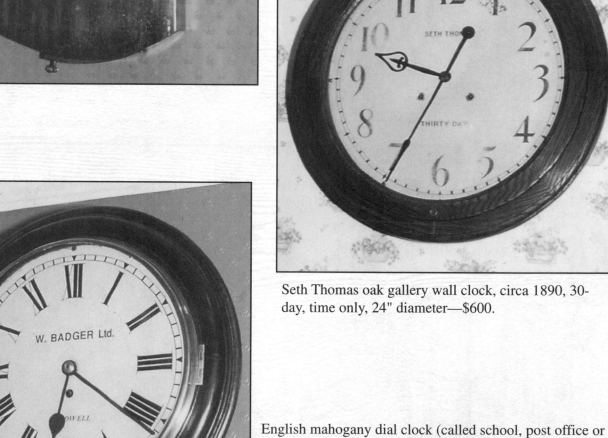

Seth Thomas oak gallery wall clock, circa 1890, 30-day, time only, 24" diameter—$600.

English mahogany dial clock (called school, post office or railroad clock), gallery type, single fusee movement; retailer's name "W. Badger Ltd." on clock's dial, eight-day, time, 12" dial diameter—$945.

Seth Thomas "Queen Ann" oak wall clock, pictured in 1881 catalogue, eight-day, time and strike, 13" wide, 36" high—$850.

German dark-stained wall clock, circa 1920, silvered dial, eight-day, time and strike, 11" wide, 25" high. Made for export trade after World War I—$345.

E.N. Welch "Eclipse" manufactured for the Metropolitan Mfg. Co., walnut wall clock, incised carving, "Eclipse" pendulum, eight-day, time, strike and alarm, 14" wide, 27-1/2" high—$550.

Label on the back of E.N. Welch, "Eclipse" wall clock. It reads, "Eclipse manufactured exclusively for Metropolitan Mfg. Co."

ECLIPSE.

MANUFACTURED EXCLUSIVELY

METROPOLITAN MFG. CO.

E.N. Welch "Office #12" oak wall clock, circa 1885, incised carving, secondhand, 30-day, time only, 23" wide, 65" high—$3,000.

E.N. Welch "Office 30-day" oak wall clock, circa 1900, incised carving, 30-day time only, 18" wide, 60" high—$2,500.

E.N. Welch "Meyerbeer" oak regulator wall clock (Meyerbeer was an Italian composer who wrote Torchlight March No. 1 in B flat), circa 1885, eight-day, time and strike, 14" wide, 40" high— $700.

Welch & Spring "#6 Regulator" rosewood wall clock, circa 1868, eight-day, time only, double weight-driven, 18" wide, 42" high—$6,800.

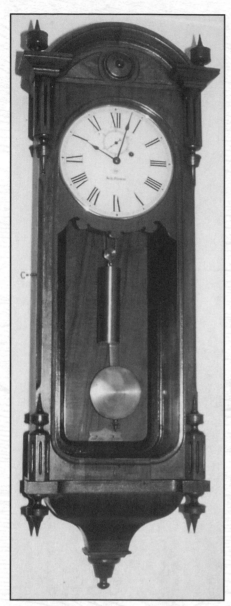

Seth Thomas "Regulator #6" oak wall clock, circa 1905, second-hand, time only, brass weight and pendulum, 16" wide, 48" high—$1,800.

Seth Thomas "Umbria" oak wall clock, 15-day time only, double-spring movement because of longer running time, 10" dial diameter, 40-1/2" high—$1,200.

German oak wall clock, circa 1890, incised carving, applied decorations, original beveled glass in door, silver metal dial and pendulum, time and strike, 12-1/2" wide, 28-1/2" high—$795.

New Haven mahogany wall clock, circa 1910, beveled glass, time and bim-bam strike on two rods, 8" wide, 24" high—$240.

Ansonia "Baghdad" oak wall clock, incised carving and applied decorations, special Ansonia silver-etched glass, time only, double weight-driven, 16" wide, 50" high—$2,000.

Welch, Spring & Co. "4 Regulator" walnut wall clock, 1873-1884, elaborately turned columns, upper finials, nickel-plated double spring movement; early model had wooden sides; later model had glass sides, 30-day time only, 16" wide, 42" high—$2,300.

Seth Thomas "Regulator No, 19" walnut wall clock, incised carving, burl decorations, mercury pendulum, metal weight, Graham dead-beat escapement, secondhand, eight-day, time only, 23" wide, 77" high—$18,000.

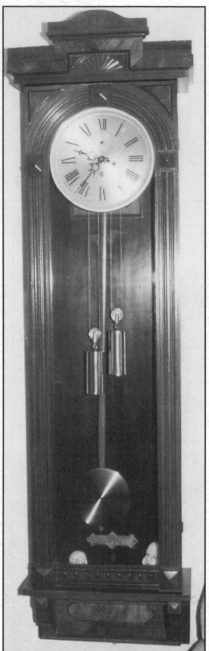

Waterbury cherry "Regulator No. 5" wall clock, burl decorations, incised carving, secondhand, brass pendulum and weights, dead-beat escapement, secondhand, glass sides, eight-day, time and strike, 19" wide, 68" high—$3,500.

Waltham oak "16 Jewelers Regulator" wall clock, circa 1895, incised carving, time only, 18" wide, 67" high. This clock hung in a Davenport, Iowa jewelry store for 90 years—$3,500.

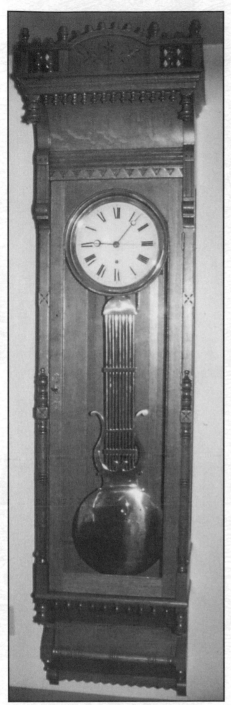

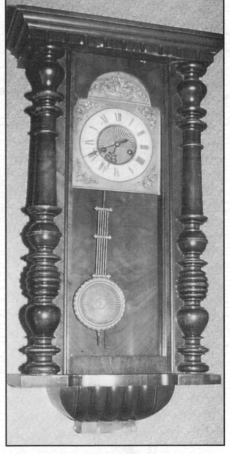

Kroeber "Jewelers Regulator #58," brass lyre pendulum, sweep secondhand, eight-day, time only, using the pinwheel type of escapement rather than the less desirable dead beat, 22" wide, 93" high—$10,000.

Schmid plastic case wall clock, circa 1950, time only, 14-1/2" high— $100.

Gustav Becker walnut wall clock, porcelain dial with brass surrounds, turned columns, time and strike, 16" wide, 33" high, runs about two weeks—no price.

Seth Thomas "Umbria" oak wall clock, secondhand, brass pendulum, 15-day time only, 40-1/2" high. There's another Umbria in this chapter—no price.

Seth Thomas "Regulator No.7" cherry wall clock, hand-carved cabinet, Graham dead-beat escapement, cut steel-pinion movement, secondhand, eight-day, time only, weight-driven, 12" dial—$6,000.

Seikosha oak wall clock, circa 1900, brass and oak pendulum, made in Tokyo, time and strike, 10" wide, 19" high—$275.

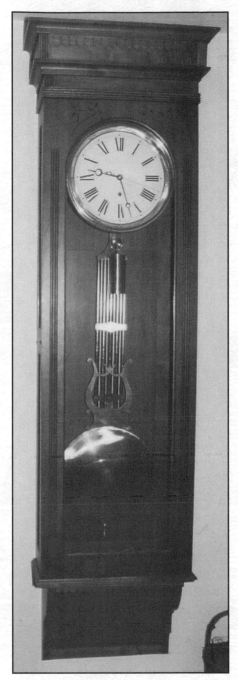

Ken Williams walnut Jeweler's Regulator wall clock, 25 to 30 years old, eight-day, time only, 21" wide, 85" high—$2,500.

German Lenzkirch walnut wall clock, circa 1880, two brass weights and a brass pendulum, original case, turned columns and finials, replaced works, eight-day, time and strike, 16" wide, 56" high—$1,000.

German walnut regulator wall clock, brass and walnut burl decorations, turned columns, three brass weights and pendulum, time and strike, 15-1/2" wide, 48" high—$1,000.

Seth Thomas "Regulator No. 63" oak wall clock, circa 1900, applied decorations, beats seconds, Graham dead-beat escapement, eight-day, time only, weight-driven, 14" dial, 76" high—$6,500.

Seth Thomas "Regulator No. 19" cherry wall clock, thumbprint mercury pendulum, sweep second-hand, Graham dead-beat escapement, eight-day, time, weight-driven, 23" wide, 75" high—$17,000.

Seth Thomas "Fine Regulator No. 10" walnut wall clock, mercury pendulum, sweep secondhand, turned side columns, burl decorations, glass sides in top section, 14" silver dial, eight-day, time only, 72" high. Some collectors consider this clock his best—$20,000.

E.N. Welch "No. 12 Regulator" walnut wall clock, incised carving, secondhand, 30-day time only, 23" wide, 65" high—$3,000.

Ansonia "Antique Hanging" cherry wall clock, brass and porcelain dial, antique brass trimmings, eight-day, time and strike, weight-driven, 46-1/2" high—$6,000.

Seth Thomas "Regulator No.6" walnut wall clock, second-hand, brass weight and pendulum, eight-day, time only, 10" dial diameter, 49" high. The 1906 catalog lists this clock available in either mahogany or oak—$2,200

Seth Thomas "Regulator No.8" cherry wall clock, secondhand, brass weight and pendulum, eight-day, time only, 14" dial, 56" high—$6,000.

Waterbury "Regulator No. 53" mahogany wall clock, incised carving, lacy hands which are common in Waterbury clocks, dead-beat escapement, eight-day, time only, double weight-driven, 19-1/2" wide, 53" high—$2,500.

Seth Thomas "Marcy" walnut wall clock, seen in 1884-1896 catalog, incised carving, eight-day, time and strike, spring-driven, 8-1/2" diameter dial, 46" high—$3,500.

Seth Thomas "Flora" oak wall clock, flower carved on clock's side, hand carving on case, eight-day, time and strike, weight-driven, 8" dial diameter, 38" high—$2,000.

Seth Thomas "Regulator No. 5" walnut wall clock (sometimes called "Miniature 16"), incised carving, glass sides, porcelain dial, eight-day, time only, weight-driven, 50" high—$7,000.

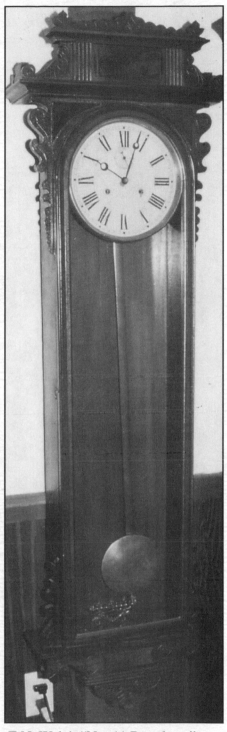

E.N. Welch "No. 11 Regulator" mahogany wall clock, secondhand, incised carving, 30-day, time only, spring-driven, 18" wide, 60" high—$2,500.

E.N. Welch "Alexis #1" rosewood ionic wall clock, 30-day movement, time only, 12" dial, 26" high. The dial has been removed to show the works—$450.

Ansonia "Queen Elizabeth" oak wall clock, awarded a prize medal at the Paris Exposition in 1878 as indicated by the label on the back of the case, eight-day, time and strike, 13-1/2" wide, 38" high—$950.

A close up of the label that reads, "Alexis Thirty Day, Time Piece, Patent Escapement."

Welch & Spring "No. 4 Regulator" walnut wall clock, circa 1880, turned columns, finials, dead-beat escapement, 30-day, time only, double spring-driven, 16" wide, 41" high— $2,400.

Seth Thomas "Regulator No.7" walnut wall clock, circa 1885, hand-carved cabinet, brass weight and pendulum, secondhand, Graham dead-beat escapement, eight-day, time only, 19" wide, 48" high—$6,500.

Seth Thomas "18 Inch Lobby" oak wall clock, secondhand, incised carving, lever movement, 15-day, time only, 25" wide, 38" high— $2,000.

Seth Thomas "Eclipse" walnut wall clock, circa 1890, incised carving, eight-day, time, strike and alarm, using Eclipse movement, 15" wide, 27" high—$500.

Bundy Time Recorder walnut wall clock, incised carving, runs 15 days, 16" wide, 55" high. The Bundy movement was by Seth Thomas. Each employee had a key number—$3,000.

Unknown maker, hanging Victorian wall clock, porcelain and brass dial, bird on clock's top, time only, 8" wide, 20" high—$350.

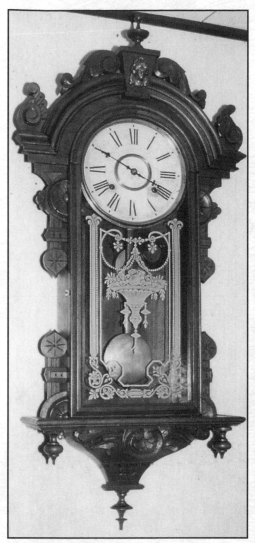

W.L. Gilbert "Columbia" walnut wall clock, circa 1886, incised carving, applied decorations, eight-day, time and strike, 17" wide, 36" high—$800.

C.H. Maur wall clock, painted porcelain dial, ormolu face and hands, 15-jewel clock with platform escapement, time only, 8" wide, 6-1/2" high—$900.

Schlenker & Kienzle German walnut wall clock, circa 1889, turned columns, finials and carved eagle on top of clock, eight-day, time and strike, 13-1/2" wide, 32" high—$600.

European walnut wall clock, circa 1880, applied decorations, turned columns, Vienna free swinger, celluloid and brass dial, time and strike, 14" wide, 33" high—$895.

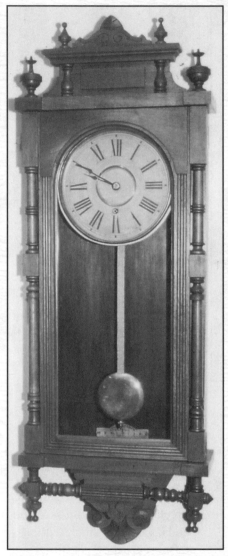

Ansonia "Queen Elizabeth" walnut wall clock, circa 1901, incised carving, eight-day, time only, 37" high—$600.

Ansonia "Queen Elizabeth" walnut wall clock, circa 1901, incised carving, eight-day, time and strike, 37" high—$700.

A display of wall clocks, including New Haven, Ithaca and Waterbury, ranging in price from $700 to $3,500.

German Junghans oak wall clock, circa 1890, eight-day, time and strike, 25" high—$385.

E.N. Welch walnut wall clock (made exclusively for Metropolitan Mfg. Co., in New York), incised carving, painted dial, eight-day, time, strike and alarm, Eclipse pendulum, 14" wide, 27" high—$450.

E. Ingraham walnut hanging kitchen wall clock, circa 1893, incised carving, thermometer and level attached to clock, 8 day time and strike, 28" high—$375.

Seth Thomas walnut hanging kitchen wall clock, circa 1890, incised carving, thermometer and level attached to clock, 8 day time and strike, 30" high—$375.

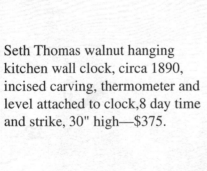

F. Kroeber walnut regulator wall clock, circa 1898, turned and reeded columns, sweep second-hand, time only, weight-driven, 53" high—$3,000.

Seth Thomas "Regulator No.30" oak wall clock, incised carving, applied decorations, time only, weight-driven, 18" wide, 48" high—$1,800.

American-made cabinet, jewelers regulator, circa 1840-1850, French works, walnut wall clock, pinwheel movement, time only, weight-driven, 20" wide, 59" high—$1,150.

English oak wall clock, circa 1880, Gothic-style, double fusee movement, cylinder pendulum, hour on a bell, 17" wide, 41" high—$3,050.

Welch, Spring & Co. "No. 4 Regulator" walnut wall clock, brass pendulum, dead-beat escapement 30-day, time only, double spring-driven 15" wide, 42" high—$1,900.

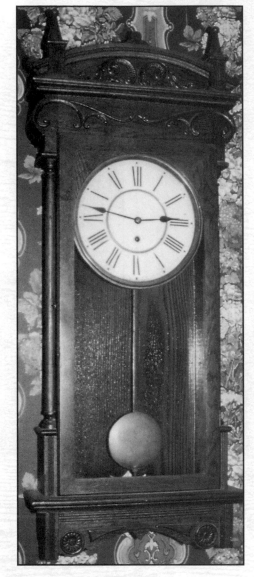

Waterbury "Cairo" oak wall clock, applied decorations, side columns, eight-day, time only, 17" wide, 42" high—$600.

Junghans walnut wall clock, circa 1890, applied decorations, turned columns, exposed brass pendulum, time and strike, 27" high—$325.

Seth Thomas rosewood pillar wall clock, prior to 1863 (Plymouth Hollow), original tablets, gilt columns, eight-day, weight-driven, 16-1/2" wide, 32" high—$500.

European Vienna Regulator walnut wall clock, circa 1880, with ebony trim, 5" diameter porcelain dial, time only, 13" wide, 34" high—$495.

W.L. Gilbert "Observatory" oak regulator wall clock, circa 1910, pressed designs and incised carving, eight-day, time only, 15-1/2" wide, 34" high—$350.

E.N. Welch "Sembirch" walnut wall clock, circa 1890, incised carving, eight-day, time only, 14" wide, 39" high—$650.

Sessions "Regulator No. 5" walnut-stained wall clock, circa 1895, incised carving, secondhand, 20" wide, 49" high, time only, double weight-driven—$3,500.

New Haven oak wall clock, circa 1920, time and strike, chime rod rather than gong, 16" wide, 31" high—$475.

Ansonia "Queen Charlotte" oak wall clock, barley-twist columns, pressed carving, eight-day, time only, 16" wide, 42" high—$600.

Junghans walnut wall clock made in Schramberg, Germany, circa 1890, called a free swingcr because the pendulum hangs free from the case, eight-day, time and strike, 13-1/2" wide, 36" high—$500.

E.N. Welch "Hanging Italian" rosewood veneer with walnut trim wall clock, sandwich glass insert in pendulum seen to the left of the case, eight-day, time and strike, 15" wide, 29" high—$900.

Waterbury oak octagonal wall clock, circa 1900, eight-day, time only, 17" wide, 24" high—$325.

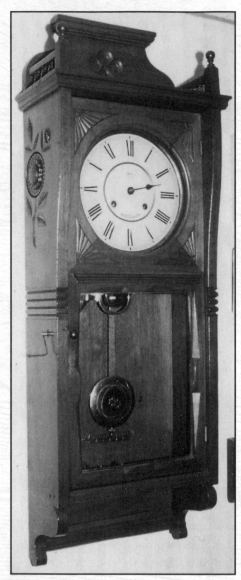

Seth Thomas "Flora" walnut wall clock, circa 1880, incised designs and carving on side panel, eight-day, time and strike, weight-driven, 13" wide, 38" high—$2,000.

New York Standard Co. oak wall clock, patented Feb. 25, 1896, originally run by a dry cell battery, 20" wide, 48" high—$1,400.

Ansonia "Regulator A" walnut octagonal wall clock, circa 1900, with ebony trim, eight-day, time and strike, 17" wide, 32" high—$450.

Japanese artificially grained octagonal wall clock, secondhand, eight-day, time and strike, 17" wide, 32" high—$295.

E.N. Welch "Verdi" rosewood octagonal wall clock, circa 1885, secondhand, eight-day, time and strike, 17" wide, 31" high—$475.

Waterbury octagonal wall clock, circa 1900-1910, eight-day, time only, 18" wide, 24" high—$325.

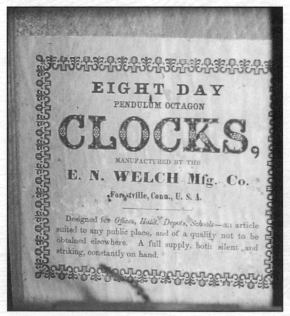

Close-up of label from E.N. Welch octagonal clock. The label reads, "Eight Day, Pendulum Octagon Clocks, Manufactured by the E.N. Welch Mfg. Co., Forestville, Conn., U.S.A. Designed for Offices, Halls, Depots, Schools an article suited to any public place, and of quality not to be obtained elsewhere. A full supply, both silent and striking, constantly on hand."

Ansonia oak miniature octagonal wall clock, circa 1910, time and strike, 12" wide, 20" high—$225.

Seth Thomas walnut octagonal wall clock with brass-applied decorations, circa 1890, time only, 16" wide, 25" high—$350.

# Chapter 10
# *Grandfather Clocks: Timely Tips*

The name "Grandfather Clock" has a friendly connotation, even though the terms long-case clock or tall-case clock, as used in England, are more descriptive. Other terms used are floor or hall clocks. This clock first appeared in England after 1600. The first ones were less than 7-feet high. Early English examples often featured an ebonized case, a hooded top, gilded ormolu mounts, a brass dial, and a narrow trunk which later became wider.

The brass dial was gradually replaced by a painted one. Marquetry and walnut veneer were popular until mahogany cases became stylish. Later, satinwood and rosewood were available. Oak, used throughout the years for less expensive clocks, appeared consistently. Some cases were plain. Others had pillars, carvings, incised lines, finials or other decorative touches. A case made of cherry and pine with satinwood inlay had a rich appearance.

Most of the early clockmakers in America were trained in England before they migrated to the New World. In the 1700s, some clockmakers on this side of the Atlantic imported movements which had to be made of metal because dampness on board ship would cause wooden works to swell and become useless. Others made their own movements. The Willard Brothers of Grafton, Massachusetts, made quality brass-movement clocks in the late 1700s. Simon Willard used enameled dials on his earliest grandfather's clocks. From about 1807-1810, Eli Terry of Connecticut made interchangeable wooden parts for inexpensive grandfather clocks that the general public could afford to buy.

At times dials were artistically designed. Roman numerals were commonly used. Since it took months to make a clock by hand, not many people could afford to buy one. Because of this, some clockmakers needed to supplement their incomes with other money-making tasks.

A grandmother clock, or a half clock, as it was sometimes called, is normally 4 feet or less in height. Brooks Palmer states this grandmother's size in one of his books with sample pictures of several. The maximum size pictured was 43" and the smallest was 36". Many of these clocks are on display in the Henry Ford Museum in Detroit. Examples were made as the 1700s ended and continued to be fashioned until the 1830s. Some were made by Boston clockmakers.

There were four types of movement that were used in the earliest American grandfather clocks. One was a 30-hour brass movement with endless chain or rope. The second was an eight-day brass movement with two weights. The final two are the 30-hour Connecticut movement and the eight-day wood movement.

Unknown maker, mahogany grandfather clock with satinwood and mother-of-pearl inlay, double weight, brass-, silver- and gold-leaf face, moving moon dial, 22" wide, 97" high—no price.

Regina music box in the lower section of the grandfather clock with five discs that have six tunes each and plays on 14 bells. Clock trips music box every hour.

European mahogany grandfather clock by Robt Thomson, circa 1840, marked "Greenock," a city in Scotland, secondhand and calendar on main dial, time and strikes on bells, 20-1/2" wide, 88" high—$3,000.

Seth Thomas mahogany custom-made, "grandfather look" floor clock, with OG upper section sitting on top of lower storage section, 30-hour, 19" wide, 77-1/2" high—$700.

View of Seth Thomas "grandfather look" clock with bottom door closed.

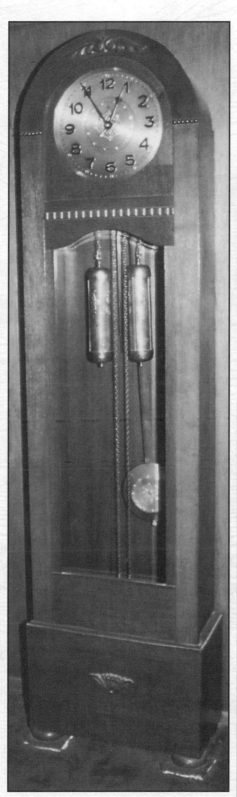

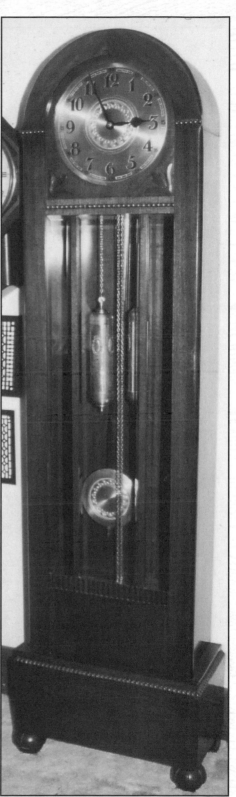

Chas. Taylor, maker, grandfather mahogany clock, Bristol area, England, circa 1830, marquetry on case, dates of month on dial, eight-day, movement, 84" high—$5,500.

Gustav Becker oak grandfather clock, circa 1900, brass pendulum, weights and face, beveled-glass door, time and strike with chimes; factory marked "Braunau Works, Bohemia, Czechoslovakia," 75" high—$1,400.

Gustav Becker mahogany grandfather clock, circa 1890, brass weights and face, beveled glass panel, 76" high—$1,800.

Face only of figured mahogany grandfather clock by Scottish maker, Andrew Dickie of Edinburgh, circa 1750, brass and silver face with "strike" and "silent" dial on upper face—$8,150.

Waltham Clock Co. mahogany grandfather clock, made from a kit, early 1900s, brass weights and pendulum, beveled glass, applied brass decorations, moon dial, 91" high—$1,400.

# Chapter 11

# *Miscellaneous Facts*

## *Early Catalog Clocks and Prices*

A sample of clocks and other clock-related items and their prices from an 1897 Sears, Roebuck & Co. catalog:

**Clocks**

Imported, nickel alarm clock, 4" dial—57 cents.

Beacon, nickel alarm clock, 6-1/2" high, 4-1/4" wide, 4" dial, New Haven Clock Company, lever movement—78 cents.

Beacon Luminous, nickel alarm clock, luminous dial, 6-1/2" high, 4-1/4" wide, 4" dial, New Haven Clock Company—97 cents.

Must Get Up, nickel alarm clock, 5-7/8" high, 4-1/2" dial, Waterbury Clock Company, large bell on the back of the clock, alarm runs five minutes with one winding, can be made to run a short, medium, long or extra long time—$1.40.

Spinning Wheel, in silver plate or gilt bronze finish, 2" dial, bevel-edged glass, 3-3/4" high, Waterbury Clock Company, good lever movement, has no alarm—$1.40.

Patrol, nickel alarm clock, 6" high, 2-1/2" dial, glass sides to show the movement, gilt front and handle, lever escapement movement, bell underneath, Waterbury Clock Company—$1.85.

Guide, nickel alarm clock, 7" high, 2-1/2" dial, glass sides show movement, gilt front and handle, bell underneath, Waterbury Clock Company—$2.

Basket, gilt bronze or silver plate, 4-7/8" high, 2" dial, beveled glass, lever movement, Water-bury Clock Company—$1.65.

Capitol, gilt or silver plate, 5-1/8" high, 2" dial, beveled glass, lever movement, Waterbury Clock Company—$2.10.

Liberty, bronze case Liberty and the Liberty Bell with trumpet and flag, 12-1/2" high, 9-1/2" wide, 3" dial, lever escapement movement—$1.85.

Cilicia, imported white porcelain case, ornamented with colors and hand-painted, height, 5" high, 5" wide, 2" dial, lever movement, New Haven Clock Company—$1.50.

Boudoir No. 19, imported white porcelain case, gilt and hand-painted decorations, 4-7/8" high, 4-3/4" diameter, 2" dial, beveled glass, lever movement, Waterbury Clock Company—$1.65.

Boudoir No. 10. genuine porcelain case, gilt and colored hand-painted decorations, 7-1/8" high, 5-3/8" long, beveled glass, 2" silver dial, lever movement, Waterbury Clock Company—$2.50.

Ardmore, imported white porcelain case, gilt and colored hand-painted decorations, 9-1/2" high, 5" wide, 2" dial, New Haven Clock Company—$3.

Boudoir No. 13, imported porcelain case, gilt and colored hand-painted decorations, 8-7/8" high, 7-1/4" long, 3-1/2" dial, Waterbury Clock Company, with alarm—$3.45.

Parlor, imported porcelain case, gilt and colored hand-painted decorations, 8-7/8" high, 7-1/4" long, 3-1/2" ivory dial, fancy gilt center, cast gilt sash and bezel eight-day, strikes hours and half hours on cup bell,

lever movement, Waterbury Clock Company—$5.75.

Bonaparte, imported porcelain case, gilt and colored hand-painted cupid decorations, 10-1/2" high, 9-3/4" wide, 3" dial, eight-day, New Haven Clock Company, strikes hours and half-hours, an elegant clock—$6.40.

Porcelain L, imported porcelain case, gilt and colored hand-painted decorations, 12" high, 10-1/2" wide, French rococo sash and porcelain dial, fine eight-day, Ansonia Clock Company, strikes hours and half hours on Cathedral gong bell—$8.25.

Dorda, polished, ebonized wood case with gilt ornaments and engraving, imitation of black onyx, 12" high, 11" long, 4-1/2" dial, eight-day, Waterbury Clock Company, strikes hours and half hours on cathedral gong bell, choice of American white dial with Roman figures or American gilt dial with Arabic figures—$4.50.

Aragon, fancy and enameled iron case, imitation of Tennessee marble, fancy colored and gilt ornamentation, 11" high, 10" wide, 6" white or gilt dial, eight-day, New Haven Clock Company, strikes hours and half hours on a cathedral gong bell—$7.50.

Savoy, French enameled iron clock with colored and gilt bronze ornamentations, 9-3/4" high, 9" wide, eight-day, Ansonia Clock Company, strikes hours and half hours on cathedral gong bell, fancy dial sash—$5.90.

Leona, fancy enameled iron case showing variegated blue finish, imitation of marble with fancy colored and gilt ornamentations, 12" high, 9-1/4" wide, 6" white or gilt dial, eight-day, New Haven Clock Company, strikes hours and half hours on cathedral gong bell—$5.95.

Castanet, fancy enameled iron case showing oak-wood finish with fancy colored and gilt ornamentations, 12-5/8" high, 8-1/2" wide, 6" dial, eight-day, New Haven Clock Company, strikes hours and halves on cathedral gong bell—$6.25.

Batavia, polished wood case in imitation of black onyx with gilt engraving, fancy bronze side ornaments and feet, fancy dial and sash, 10-1/2" high, 11-3/4" long, 5-1/2" dial, eight-day, Waterbury Clock Company, strikes hours and halves on cathedral gong bell with American gilt or white dial—$4.40.

Dover, polished wood case in imitation of black onyx, fancy gilt engraving, 10-1/4" high, 9-1/2" wide, fancy American sash and dial, eight-day, Ansonia Clock Company, strikes hours and halves on cathedral gong bell—$4.85 (with visible escapement, add 30 cents).

New Monaco, fancy enameled iron case, smoked finish, imitation of marble with fancy colored and gilt decorations, 11-1/2" high, 12" wide, 6" white or gilt dial, eight-day, New Haven Clock Company, strikes hours and halves on cathedral gong bell—$7.80.

Amiens, enameled iron case with fancy colored and gilt ornamentations and feet, 10-1/4" high, 13-1/2" wide, gilt dial and sash, eight-day, Ansonia Clock Company, strikes hours and halves on cathedral gong bell—$7.90.

Fresno, polished wood case in imitation of black onyx, fancy

gilt engraving, marbleized columns with gilt bronze bases and caps, fancy sash, 10-3/8" high, 16" long, 5-1/2" dial, eight-day, Waterbury Clock Company, strikes hours and halves on cathedral gong bell, American white dial, Roman figures or American gilt dial with Arabic figures—$5.40.

Chester, polished wood case in imitation of black onyx with gilt engraving, gilt bronze side ornaments and feet, fancy sash, 10-1/2" high, 16" wide, eight-day, Ansonia Clock Company, strikes hours and halves on cathedral gong bell, fine American gilt dial with Arabic figures—$6.60.

Java, polished wood case in imitation of black onyx, fancy gilt engraving, six marbleized columns with artistic bronze caps and bases, large fancy bronze side ornaments and feet, 11-1/4" high, 18-1/4" long, 5-1/2" dial, eight-day, Waterbury Clock Company, strikes hours and halves on cathedral gong bell, American white dial with Roman figures or fancy gilt dial with Arabic figures—$6.30.

Marble, polished wood case in imitation of brown Italian or verde antique (green) marble-top base and columns with imitation black onyx body, fancy gilt engraving with gilt bronze ornaments and tops and bases to columns, also heavy bronze side ornaments and feet, 17" long, 11-1/4" high; top is ornamented by beautiful gilt bronze figure of lady and harp, 8-1/2" high, eight-day movement, Waterbury Clock Company, strikes hours and halves on cathedral gong bell, gilt dial with Arabic figures in black enamel, has a patent regulator by which the clock can be regulated without touching the

pendulum—$6.45.

12 different cabinet clocks, solid oak or black walnut, 22" to 24-1/2" high, 6" to 8" dials, eight-day, strikes hours and halves on cathedral gong bell or wire bell; from New Haven Clock Company, Ansonia Clock Company and Waterbury Clock Company; models are Duxbury, Beaver, Saranac, Flint, Clarence, Buffalo, Niantic, Richland, Triumph, Recorder, King and Monarch—$2 to $6.15

**Ornaments for mantels or tops of mantel clocks**

Ceres, bronze statue of lady with bundle of wheat and sickle 7" high, 7-7/8" long—$1.90.

Ormonde, bronze figure of horse, 7-1/2" high, 8" long—$1.75.

Pointer, bronze ornament, 4" high, 7-3/8" long—95 cents.

# Patent Numbers and Dates Issued

| Year | Number |
|------|-------:|
| 1836 | 1 |
| 1837 | 110 |
| 1838 | 516 |
| 1839 | 1,061 |
| 1840 | 1,465 |
| 1841 | 1,923 |
| 1842 | 2,413 |
| 1843 | 2,901 |
| 1844 | 3,395 |
| 1845 | 3,873 |
| 1846 | 4,348 |
| 1847 | 4,914 |
| 1848 | 5,409 |
| 1849 | 5,993 |
| 1850 | 6,981 |
| 1851 | 7,865 |
| 1852 | 8,622 |
| 1853 | 9,512 |
| 1854 | 10,358 |
| 1855 | 12,117 |
| 1856 | 14,009 |
| 1857 | 16,324 |
| 1858 | 19,010 |
| 1859 | 22,477 |
| 1860 | 26,642 |
| 1861 | 31,005 |
| 1862 | 34,045 |
| 1863 | 37,266 |
| 1864 | 41,047 |
| 1865 | 45,685 |
| 1866 | 51,784 |
| 1867 | 60,658 |
| 1868 | 72,959 |
| 1869 | 85,503 |
| 1870 | 98,460 |
| 1871 | 110,617 |
| 1872 | 122,304 |
| 1873 | 134,504 |
| 1874 | 145,120 |
| 1875 | 158,350 |
| 1876 | 171,641 |
| 1877 | 185,813 |
| 1878 | 198,733 |
| 1879 | 211,078 |
| 1880 | 223,211 |
| 1881 | 236,137 |
| 1882 | 251,685 |
| 1883 | 269,820 |
| 1884 | 291,016 |
| 1885 | 310,163 |
| 1886 | 333,494 |

| Year | Number |
|------|-------:|
| 1887 | 355,291 |
| 1888 | 375,720 |
| 1889 | 395,305 |
| 1890 | 418,665 |
| 1891 | 443,987 |
| 1892 | 466,315 |
| 1893 | 488,976 |
| 1894 | 511,744 |
| 1895 | 531,619 |
| 1896 | 552,502 |
| 1897 | 574,369 |
| 1898 | 596,467 |
| 1899 | 616,871 |
| 1900 | 640,167 |
| 1901 | 664,827 |
| 1902 | 690,385 |
| 1903 | 717,521 |
| 1904 | 748,567 |
| 1905 | 778,834 |
| 1906 | 808,618 |
| 1907 | 839,799 |
| 1908 | 875,679 |
| 1909 | 908,436 |
| 1910 | 945,010 |
| 1911 | 980,178 |
| 1912 | 1,013,095 |
| 1913 | 1,049,326 |
| 1914 | 1,083,267 |
| 1915 | 1,123,212 |
| 1916 | 1,166,419 |
| 1917 | 1,210,389 |
| 1918 | 1,251,458 |
| 1919 | 1,290,027 |
| 1920 | 1,326,899 |
| 1921 | 1,364,063 |
| 1922 | 1,401,948 |
| 1924 | 1,478,996 |
| 1925 | 1,521,590 |
| 1926 | 1,568,040 |
| 1927 | 1,612,790 |
| 1928 | 1,654,521 |
| 1929 | 1,696,897 |
| 1930 | 1,742,181 |
| 1931 | 1,787,424 |
| 1932 | 1,839,190 |
| 1933 | 1,892,663 |
| 1934 | 1,944,449 |
| 1935 | 1,985,878 |
| 1936 | 2,026,510 |
| 1937 | 2,066,309 |
| 1938 | 2,101,004 |
| 1939 | 2,142,080 |

| Year | Number |
|---|---|
| 1940 | 2,185,170 |
| 1941 | 2,227,418 |
| 1942 | 2,268,540 |
| 1943 | 2,307,007 |
| 1944 | 2,338,081 |
| 1945 | 2,366,154 |
| 1946 | 2,391,856 |
| 1947 | 2,413,675 |
| 1948 | 2,433,824 |
| 1949 | 2,457,797 |
| 1950 | 2,492,944 |
| 1951 | 2,536,016 |
| 1952 | 2,580,379 |
| 1953 | 2,624,016 |
| 1954 | 2,664,562 |
| 1955 | 2,698,431 |
| 1956 | 2,728,913 |
| 1957 | 2,775,762 |
| 1958 | 2,813,567 |
| 1959 | 2,866,973 |

## *English Design Registry Numbers: 1885-1946*

*(Chart gives registry # issued each year)*

| Year | Number |
|---|---|
| 1885 | 20,000 |
| 1886 | 40,800 |
| 1887 | 64,700 |
| 1888 | 91,800 |
| 1889 | 117,800 |
| 1890 | 142,300 |
| 1891 | 164,000 |
| 1892 | 186,400 |
| 1893 | 206,100 |
| 1894 | 225,000 |
| 1895 | 248,200 |
| 1896 | 268,800 |
| 1897 | 291,400 |

| Year | Number |
|---|---|
| 1898 | 311,677 |
| 1899 | 332,200 |
| 1900 | 351,600 |
| 1901 | 368,186 |
| 1902 | 385,180 |
| 1903 | 403,200 |
| 1904 | 424,400 |
| 1905 | 447,800 |
| 1906 | 471,860 |
| 1907 | 493,900 |
| 1908 | 518,640 |
| 1909 | 535,170 |
| 1910 | Not available |
| 1911 | 575,817 |
| 1912 | 594,195 |
| 1913 | 612,431 |
| 1914 | 630,190 |
| 1915 | 644,935 |
| 1916 | 653,521 |
| 1917 | 658,988 |
| 1918 | 662,872 |
| 1919 | 666,128 |
| 1920 | 673,750 |
| 1921 | 680,147 |
| 1922 | 687,144 |
| 1923 | 694,999 |
| 1924 | 702,671 |
| 1925 | 710,165 |
| 1926 | 718,057 |
| 1927 | 726,330 |
| 1928 | 734,370 |
| 1929 | 742,725 |
| 1930 | 751,160 |
| 1931 | 760,583 |
| 1932 | 769,670 |
| 1933 | 779,292 |
| 1934 | 789,019 |
| 1935 | 799,097 |
| 1936 | 808,794 |
| 1937 | 817,293 |
| 1938 | 825,231 |
| 1939 | 832,610 |
| 1940 | 837,520 |
| 1941 | 838,590 |
| 1942 | 839,220 |
| 1943 | 839,980 |
| 1944 | 841,040 |
| 1945 | 842,670 |
| 1946 | 845,550 |

# *Calendar Clock Inventors*

| Inventor | Residence | Patent Date |
|---|---|---|
| Randal T. Andrews | Thomason, CT | Feb. 15, 1876 |
| William H. Atkins | Ithaca, NY | Sept. 19, 1854 |
| Alfonzo Boardman | Forestville, CT | July 2, 1867 |
| Charles M. Clinton | Ithaca, NY | June 25, 1867 |
| Alfred A. Cowles | New York, NY | July 13, 1875 |
| Charles W. Feishtinger | Fritztown, PA | Oct. 9, 1894 |
| Benjamin Franklin | Chicago, IL | June 12, 1883 |
| David J. Gale | Sheboygan, WI | June 19, 1877 |
| | | April 21, 1885 |
| John H.H. Hawes | Ithaca, NY | May 17, 1853 |
| Henry B. Horton | Ithaca, NY | April 18, 1865 |
| | | Aug. 28, 1866 |
| F. Kroeber | Hoboken, NJ | July 31, 1877 |
| Benjamin B. Lewis | Bristol, CT | Feb. 4, 1862 |
| | | June 21, 1864 |
| | | Dec. 29, 1868 |
| | | Nov. 15, 1881 |
| T.W.R. McCabe | Winston, CT | Nov. 10, 1896 |
| Galusha Maranville | Winston, CT | March 5, 1861 |
| James E. & Eugene M. Mix | Bristol, CT | April 4, 1862 |
| Don J. Mozart/Levi Beach | New York, NY | Jan. 5, 1864 |
| George B. Owen | New York, NY | April 24, 1866 |
| John I. Peatfield | Arlington, MA | July 15, 1902 |
| Albert Phelps | Ansonia, CT | Dec. 5, 1876 |
| Henry S. Prentiss | New York, NY | April 14, 1891 |
| Josiah K. Seem | Canton, PA | Jan. 7, 1868 |
| | Macomb, IL | Dec. 24, 1872 |
| | | Dec. 13, 1881 |
| William A. Terry | Bristol, CT | June 16, 1868 |
| | | Jan 25, 1870 |
| | | July 13, 1875 |
| A.F. Wells | Friendship, NY | July 30, 1889 |
| James E. Young | Genoa, NY | June 19, 1883 |

# Glossary

**Acorn clock**: A clock whose shape resembles an acorn.

**Adamantine**: A patented colored celluloid applied as veneer that looks like marble. A Seth Thomas-exclusive process.

**Advertising clock**: A clock used for promotional purposes on which the advertising may be found on the case, dial or tablet.

**Alarm**: An attachment to a clock that rings or gongs at a pre-selected time.

**Animated clock**: A clock that incorporates a lifelike movement characteristic of an animal or person.

**Anniversary clock**: A clock, wound annually, that runs for a full year. Sometimes called a 400-day clock.

**Apron**: A decorative piece, sometimes used to hide construction details. It may be on the bottom of a case or between the legs of a floor or shelf clock.

**Arabic numerals**: Figures on a dial written 1, 2, 3, etc.

**Arc**: The swinging path of a clock pendulum.

**Backboard**: The inside back of a clock case where a label was frequently applied.

**Balance**: The oscillating wheel that, along with the hairspring, regulates the speed of a clock.

**Banjo clock**: The name given to Simon Willard's "Improved Timepiece" (a wall clock), because of its banjo shape. Willard introduced it around 1800.

**Barrel**: A round container that houses the main spring.

**Beading**: A type of carved or applied molding resembling beads.

**Beat**: The ticking sound of a clock. When the ticking is consistently steady, it is "in beat." If it is irregular, it is "out of beat."

**Beehive clock**: A clock with a rounded case that bears some resemblance to a beehive.

**Bevel**: A chamfer, such as the angled edge on plate glass.

**Bezel**: A ring of wood or metal that surrounds and holds the glass over the clock dial.

**Black clocks**: Clocks made of marble, black iron or black-enameled wood, popular from about 1880 to 1920.

**Blacks**: The term used to refer to imitation marble clocks.

**Blinking eye**: Eyes on clocks that winked with the movement of the escapement to which they were connected. The Little Sambo clock is an example of such a clock with winking eyes.

**Bob**: The weight at the bottom end of a pendulum rod.

**Bracket clock**: The British name for a shelf clock.

**Brass works**: A clock mechanism made of brass.

**Calendar clock**: A clock that can indicate the day, month and date or combinations thereof, as well as the time. A perpetual calendar makes provisions for the various lengths of months and adjusts accordingly, whereas a simple calendar must be changed manually to accommodate a change from a 30-day to a 31-day month.

**Camel back**: A term used to describe a mantel clock, rounded high in the center and flat on the ends. Also called "Hump back or Tambour."

**Carriage clock**: This clock is sometimes called a traveling clock.

**Case**: The housing for the works of a clock.

**Celluloid**: A trade name for the first artificial plastic, invented in 1869, that received wide commercial use. Some clock cases in the early 1900s were made of this highly flammable material.

**Chamfer**: A slope or angled edge on wood or plate glass, a bevel.

**China or porcelain**: A clock with a case made of glazed porcelain.

**Clock**: A machine that records the passing of time and strikes at least on the hour.

**Cornice**: The horizontal molded projection at the top a clock case.

**Cottage clock**: A flat-top clock without a handle.

**Crystal regulator**: A shelf clock with glass panels on all four sides.

**Date dial**: An additional clock dial that shows the dates of the month.

**Dead-beat escapement**: A clock escapement that does not recoil (fall back).

**Dial**: A clock's face with numbers and hands.

**Drum**: A round barrel about which the weight cord is wound.

**Ebonized**: A black finish that looks like ebony wood.

**Eight-day clock**: A clock that runs for eight days on one winding.

**Escapement**: The clock mechanism that controls the

swing of the pendulum or the movement of the balance wheel.

**Escutcheon**: The trim around a key hole.

**Finial**: A wooden or metal spire or turning often on the top of a clock case.

**Fly**: This, located on the strike train, slows down the striking rate.

**Flying pendulum**: A novelty clock invented in 1883 and made again in the late 1950s. Hanging from an arm, a small ball on a thread swings in a horizontal circle and is regulated by twisting and untwisting around vertical rods on each side of the clock. Also referred to as "Ignatz."

**Four-hundred day**: A clock, wound annually, that runs for a full year.

**Frame**: The case of a clock.

**Fusee or fuzee**: A grooved cone upon which the cord from the spring container unwinds to equalize the force of the spring in a clock.

**Gallery clock**: An eight-day or electric clock with a simple case and a dial usually 8" or larger that hung on the wall in a public establishment.

**Gilt**: A gold-colored coating.

**Gimbal**: A support which keeps a timekeeper level.

**Girandole**: The American wall clock designed by Lemuel Curtis.

**Gold leaf**: Extremely thin sheet of solid gold sometime applied as a decoration on columns, tablets or other parts of a clock case.

**Gothic case**: A case, a variation of a steeple clock, with a pointed top that bears a resemblance to Gothic architecture.

**Grandfather clock**: The name for a floor-standing clock in a tall, upright case. Originally called a long-case or tall-case clock.

**Grandmother clock**: A smaller floor-standing version of a grandfather clock.

**Hair-spring**: A slender hair-like coil that controls the regular movement of the balance wheel in a clock.

**Hands**: The time indicators that mark the hours, minutes or seconds on a clock dial.

**Hanging shelf-clock**: A wall clock with a shelf-like base that makes it appear as if is sitting on a shelf.

**Horology**: The science of measuring time or making timepieces.

**Ignatz**: A novelty clock invented in 1883 and made again in the late 1950s. Hanging from an arm, a small ball on a thread swings in a horizontal circle and is regulated by twisting and untwisting around vertical rods on each side of the clock.

**Interchangeable parts**: Parts that can be used in any machine of the same model.

**Ionic**: A clock having a configuration of an "8."

**Iron-front**: A shelf clock with a cast-iron front.

**Kidney dial**: A dial on a clock that resembles the shape of a kidney.

**Kitchen clock**: A clock frequently of oak, manufactured from the late 1800s to the early 1900s, that sat on a shelf in the kitchen.

**Labels**: Pieces of paper, used inside a clock case, originally as a dust protector. Later, they were used as an advertisement of the maker's product, listing such things as place of manufacture, manufacturer and how to operate the clock.

**Long-case clock**: The original name for a grandfather clock.

**Looking-glass clock**: A clock with a box-like case and mirror instead of a painted glass tablet.

**Lyre clock**: The clock style devised by Aaron Willard Jr. of Boston.

**Mainspring**: The principal or driving power that keeps the mechanism running in a spring-driven clock.

**Mantel clock**: A shelf clock.

**Marine or lever clocks**: Clocks that operate with a hair-spring balance and continue to run when transported or set on an uneven surface (contrary to pendulum clocks). Often used aboard ships.

**Mask**: A human or animal face used as a decoration.

**Medallion**: An applied circular, oval or square decorative turning used on a clock case.

**Mercury pendulum**: In American clocks, a silvery-looking, usually cylindrical, pendulum that resembles French examples, except that the French version actually contained mercury.

**Mirror clock**: See "Looking glass."

**Mission style**: A straight-lined, plain clock case that was popular from about 1900 to 1925, when mission's solid, stocky furniture was made.

**Molding**: A continuous decorative edging.

**Movement**: The "works" of a clock.

**Novelty clock**: A small, often animated, clock usually in the shape of a familiar object that may perform some unusual task, like lighting a cigarette.

**OG or ogee**: A double, continuous S-like curve used as

a molding on certain straight, rectangular clocks of the early 1800s.

**Open escapement**: The wheel and pallet movement that can be seen on some clock dials.

**Ormolu**: Brass castings, an alloy of zinc and copper, with gilt plating used as case decorations. Used extensively in France.

**Pallet**: A catching device that regulated the speed of a clock by releasing one notch of a toothed wheel (ratchet wheel) at each swing of the pendulum or turn of the balance wheel.

**Papier-mâché**: Mashed paper that was mixed with glue and other material that could be formed into various shapes. Used for clock cases in the middle 1800s, principally by the Litchfield Manufacturing Co., of Litchfield, Connecticut.

**Parlor clock**: The older, carved-case (often walnut) Victorian clock of the mid- to late 1800s that stood on a shelf or mantel in the parlor, as opposed to a shelf clock of pressed oak or simpler designed walnut from the 1890s or early 1900s.

**Pediment**: An ornamental top on a clock case, frequently curved in shape.

**Pendulum**: A clock weight, often ornamental, hung from a fixed point so as to swing to and fro as it regulates the clock's movement.

**Perpetual**: A clock that can indicate the day, month and date or combinations thereof, as well as the time. It makes provisions for the various lengths of months and adjusts accordingly.

**Pillar & scroll**: A shelf clock whose design was devised by Eli Terry.

**Regulator clock**: Originally a term for an accurate clock. Later, it became a name used to designate some wall clocks.

**Reverse painting**: A picture or design often used on a clock tablet and painted on the back side of a glass in reverse order of a normal painting.

**Rococo**: An early 19th century florid style used on furniture and clocks in excessiveness. In the style of Louis XIV and Louis XV.

**Roman numerals**: Roman letters used as numerals on clock dials, as in I, II, III, IV, etc. On older clocks, four was often represented by IIII, an old Roman numeral for IV. It is said that this form better balances the VIII on the other side of the dial.

**Salisbury clock**: The oldest surviving mechanical clock

in England.

**Serpentine**: The alternating of concave and convex curves on the front of an object.

**Shelf clock**: A clock designed to sit on a shelf or mantel.

**Simple calendar**: This clock has an extra hand that points to the day of the month. See "Calendar clock."

**Spandrels**: The four corners, featuring painted designs or metal decorations, that square-off a round clock dial.

**Spring clock**: A clock whose power is provided by springs.

**Steeple clock**: A clock with a sharply pointed Gothic case and finials at each side.

**TP**: An abbreviation for time piece.

**T&S**: An abbreviation for time and strike.

**Tablet**: The front, lower glass, frequently painted, on a clock case.

**Tall clock**: A long-case, floor clock, often called a grandfather clock.

**Tambour clock**: A shelf clock, also called a humpback or camelback clock, with a case that is flat at each side and rounded in the middle.

**30-day clock**: A clock that requires winding once a month.

**30-hour clock**: A clock that runs for 30 hours without rewinding.

**Time and strike**: A clock that both tells the time and strikes or chimes.

**Timepiece**: A clock that tells time only and does not strike or chime.

**Tower clock**: A clock found in he tower of a public building.

**Visible escapement**: The wheel and pallet movement that can be seen on some clock dials.

**Wagon spring**: A series of flat springs, attributed to Joseph Ives of Bristol, Connecticut, that are used instead of a coil spring to power the clock movement.

**Wall clock**: A clock that hangs on the wall.

**Weights**: The power source that drives the mechanism in a clock when it is not spring-driven.

**Zebrawood**: An African wood, straw-colored with fine stripes, that is sliced into veneers to cover a base wood. Also called zebrano.

# *Bibliography*

**Books**

*A Treasury of American Clocks*, New York: The Macmillan Company: 1967.

Bailey, Chris H., *Two Hundred Years of American Clocks and Watches*, Englewood Cliffs: A Rutledge Book, Prentice-Hall: no date.

Brewer, Clifford, *Pocket Book of Clocks*, Country Life Books, an imprint of Newes Books, a division of the Hamlyn Publishing Group Ltd., Felthan, Middlesex, England: 1983.

Burton, Eric, *Clocks and Watches 1400-1900*, Frederick A. Praeger, Publishers, New York and Washington, no date.

Drepperd, Carl W., *Americana Clocks and Clockmakers*, The Country Life Press, Garden City, NY: 1947.

Ehrhardt, Roy and Red Rabeneck, *Clock Identification and Price Guide*, Heart of America Press, Kansas City, MO: 1983.

Lloyd, Alan H., *The Collector's Dictionary of Clocks*, A.S. Barnes and Co., New York, NY: 1964.

Ly, Tran Duy, *Clocks: A Guide to Identification and Prices*, Arlington, VA: 1984.

Maust, Don, ed., *Early American Clocks*, E.G. Warman Publishing Co., Union Town, PA: 1971.

Moore, Hudson N., *The Old Clock Book*, Tudor Publishing Company, New York, NY: 1911, March 1936.

Palmer, Brooks, *The Book of American Clocks*, The Macmillan Company, New York, NY: 1950.

Schwartz, Marvin D., *Collectors' Guide to Antique American Clocks*, Doubleday & Company, Inc., Garden City, NY: 1975.

Smith, Alan, ed., *The International Dictionary of Clocks*, London and Auckland: Melbourne, Singapore and Toronto: 1988.

Welch, Kenneth F., *The History of Clocks and Watches*, Drake Publishers, Inc., New York, NY: 1972.

**Catalogs**

"F. Kroeber Clock Co. Manufactures, Catalogue of Clocks," New York, NY: 1898-1899.

Israel, Fred L., ed., "1897 Sears, Roebuck Catalogue," Chelsea House Publishers, New York, NY: 1976.

**Newsletters**

"Eli Terry: Dreamer, Artisan and Clockmaker," Bulletin of the National Association of Watch and Clock Collectors, Inc., Summer 1965.

"The Welch, Spring and Company," Bulletin of the National Association of Watch and Clock Collectors, Inc., #12, February 1978.

# Photo Index